GENESIS to REVELATION

A Comprehensive Verse-by-Verse Exploration of the Bible

REVELATION

C. M. KEMPTON HEWITT

LEADER GUIDE

GENESIS to REVELATION

A Comprehensive Verse-by-Verse Exploration of the Bible

REVELATION
C. M. KEMPTON HEWITT

LEADER GUIDE

GENESIS TO REVELATION SERIES:
REVELATION
LEADER GUIDE

ISBN 9781501855443

Manufactured in the United States of America
18 19 20 21 22 23 24 25 26 27—10 9 8 7 6 5 4 3 2 1

ABINGDON PRESS
Nashville

HOW TO TEACH GENESIS TO REVELATION

Unique Features of This Bible Study

In Genesis to Revelation, you and your class will study the Bible in three steps. Each step provides a different level of understanding of the Scripture. We call these steps Dimension One, Dimension Two, and Dimension Three.

Dimension One concerns what the Bible actually says. You do not interpret the Scripture at this point; you merely take account of what it says. Your main goal for this dimension is to get the content of the passage clear in your mind. What does the Bible say?

Dimension One is in workbook form. The members of the class will write the answers to questions about the passage in the space provided in the participant book. All the questions in Dimension One can be answered by reading the Bible itself. Be sure the class finishes Dimension One before going on to Dimensions Two and Three.

Dimension Two concerns information that will shed light on the Scripture under consideration. Dimension Two will answer such questions as

- What are the original meanings of some of the words used in the passage?

- What is the original background of the passage?

- Why was the passage most likely written?

- What are the relationships between the persons mentioned in the passage?

- What geographical and cultural factors affect the meaning of the passage?

The question for Dimension Two is, What information do we need in order to understand the meaning of the passage? In Dimension One the class members will discover what the Bible says. In Dimension Two they will discover what the Bible means.

Dimension Three focuses on interpreting the Scripture and applying it to life situations. The questions here are

- What is the meaning of the passage for my life?

- What response does the passage require of me as a Christian?

- What response does this passage require of us as a group?

Dimension Three questions have no easy answers. The task of applying the Scripture to life situations is up to you and the class.

Aside from the three-dimensional approach, another unique feature of this study is the organization of the series as a whole. Classes that choose to study the Genesis to Revelation Series will be able to study all the books of the Bible in their biblical order. This method will give the class continuity that is not present in most other Bible studies. The class will read and study virtually every verse of the Bible, from Genesis straight through to Revelation.

Weekly Preparation

Begin planning for each session early in the week. Read the passage that the lesson covers, and write the answers to Dimension One questions in the participant book. Then read Dimensions Two and Three in the participant book. Make a note of any questions or comments you have. Finally, study the material in the leader guide carefully. Decide how you want to organize your class session.

Organizing the Class Session

Since Genesis to Revelation involves three steps in studying the Scripture, you will want to organize your class sessions around these three dimensions. Each lesson in the participant book and this leader guide consists of three parts.

The first part of each lesson in the leader guide is the same as the Dimension One section in the participant book, except that the leader guide includes the answers to Dimension One questions. These questions and answers are taken from the New International Version of the Bible.

You might use Dimension One in several ways:

1. Ask the group members to read the Scripture and to write the answers to all the Dimension One questions before coming to class. This method will require that the class covenant to spend the necessary amount of study time outside of class. When the class session begins, read through the Dimension One questions, asking for responses from the group members. If anyone needs help with any of the answers, look at the biblical reference together.

2. Or, if you have enough class time, you might spend the first part of the session working through the Dimension One questions together as a group. Locate the Scripture references, ask the questions one at a time, and invite the class members to find the answers and to read them aloud. Then allow enough time for them to write the answers in the participant book.

3. Or, take some time at the beginning of the class session for group members to work individually. Have them read the Dimension One questions and the Scripture references and then write their answers to the questions in the spaces provided in the participant book. Discuss together any questions or answers in Dimension One that do not seem clear. This approach may take longer than the others, but it provides a good change of pace from time to time.

You do not have to organize your class sessions the same way every week. Ask the class members what they prefer. Experiment! You may find ways to study the Dimension One material other than the ones listed above.

The second part of each lesson in this leader guide corresponds to the second part of the participant book lessons. The Dimension Two section of the participant book provides background information to help the participants understand the Scripture. Become familiar with the information in the participant book.

Dimension Two of this leader guide contains additional information on the passage. The leader guide goes into more depth with some parts of the passage than the participant book does. You will want to share this information with the group in whatever way seems appropriate. For example, if someone raises a question about a particular verse, share any additional background information from the leader guide.

You might raise a simple question such as, What words or phrases gave you trouble in understanding the passage? or, Having grasped the content of the passage, what questions remain in your mind? Encourage the group members to share confusing points, troublesome words or phrases, or lingering questions. Write these problems on a posterboard or markerboard. This list of concerns will form the outline for the second portion of the session.

These concerns may also stimulate some research on the part of the group members. If your study group is large enough, divide the class into three groups. Then divide the passage for the following week into three parts. Assign a portion of the passage to each group. Using Bible commentaries and Bible dictionaries, direct each group to discover as much as it can about this portion of the passage before the class meets again. Each group will then report its findings during the class session.

The third part of each lesson in this leader guide relates to Dimension Three in the participant book. This section helps class members discover how to apply the Scripture to their own lives. Here you will find one or more interpretations of the passage—whether traditional, historical, or contemporary. Use these interpretations when appropriate to illumine the passage for the group members.

Dimension Three in the participant book points out some of the issues in the passage that are relevant to our lives. For each of these issues, the participant book raises questions to help the participants assess the meaning of the Scripture for their lives. The information in Dimension Three of the leader guide is designed to help you lead the class in discussing these issues. Usually, you will find a more in-depth discussion of portions of the Scripture.

The discussion in the leader guide will give you a better perspective on the Scripture and its interpretation before you begin to assess its meaning for today. You will probably want to share this Dimension Three information with the class to open the discussion. For each life situation, the leader guide contains suggestions on facilitating the class discussion. You, as the leader, are responsible for group discussions of Dimension Three issues.

Assembling Your Materials

You will need at least three items to prepare for and conduct each class session:

- A leader guide

- A participant book

- A Bible—you may use any translation or several; the answers in this leader guide are taken from the New International Version.

One advantage of the Genesis to Revelation Series is that the study is self-contained. That is, all you need to lead this Bible study is provided for you in the participant books and leader guides. Occasionally, or perhaps on a regular basis, you might want to consult other sources for additional information.

HOW TO LEAD A DISCUSSION

The Teacher as Discussion Leader

As the leader of this series or a part of this series, one of your main responsibilities during each class period will be to lead the class discussion. Some leaders are apprehensive about leading a discussion. In many ways, it is easier to lecture to the class. But remember that the class members will surely benefit more from the class sessions when they actively participate in a discussion of the material.

Leading a discussion is a skill that any teacher can master with practice. And keep in mind—especially if your class is not used to discussion—that the members of your group will also be learning through practice. The following are some pointers on how to lead interesting and thought-provoking discussions in the study group.

Preparing for a Discussion—Where Do I Start?

1. Focus on the subject that will be discussed and on the goal you want to achieve through that discussion.

2. Prepare by collecting information and data that you will need; jot down these ideas, facts, and questions so that you will have them when you need them.

3. Begin organizing your ideas; stop often to review your work. Keep in mind the climate within the group—attitudes, feelings, eagerness to participate and learn.

4. Consider possible alternative group procedures. Be prepared for the unexpected.

5. Having reached your goal, think through several ways to bring the discussion to a close.

As the leader, do not feel that your responsibility is to give a full account or report of the assigned material. This practice promotes dependency. Instead, through stimulating questions and discussion, the participants will read the material—not because you tell them to but because they want to read and prepare.

How Do I Establish a Climate for Learning?

The leader's readiness and preparation quickly establish a climate in which the group can proceed and its members learn and grow. The anxiety and fear of an unprepared leader are contagious but so are the positive vibrations coming from a leader who is prepared to move into a learning enterprise.

An attitude of shared ownership is also basic. Group members need to perceive themselves as part of the learning experience. Persons establish ownership by working on goals, sharing concerns, and accepting major responsibility for learning.

Here are several ways the leader can foster a positive climate for learning and growth.

1. Readiness. A leader who is always fully prepared can promote, in turn, the group's readiness to learn.

2. Exploration. When the leader encourages group members to freely explore new ideas, persons will know they are in a group whose primary function is learning.

3. Exposure. A leader who is open, honest, and willing to reveal himself or herself to the group will encourage participants to discuss their feelings and opinions.

4. Confidentiality. A leader can create a climate for learning when he or she respects the confidentiality of group members and encourages the group members to respect one another's confidentiality.

5. Acceptance. When a leader shows a high degree of acceptance, participants can likewise accept one another honestly.

How Can I Deal With Conflict?

What if conflict or strong disagreement arises in your group? What do you do? Think about the effective and ineffective ways you have dealt with conflict in the past.

Group conflict may come from one of several sources. One common source of conflict involves personality clashes. Any group is almost certain to contain at least two persons whose personalities clash. If you break your class into smaller groups for discussion, be sure these persons are in separate groups.

Another common source of group conflict is subject matter. The Bible can be a very controversial subject. Remember the difference between discussion or disagreement and conflict. As a leader you will have to decide when to encourage discussion and when to discourage conflict that is destructive to the group process.

Group conflict may also come from a general atmosphere conducive to expression of ideas and opinions. Try to discourage persons in the group from being judgmental toward others and their ideas. Keep reminding the class that each person is entitled to his or her own opinions and that no one opinion is more valid than another.

How Much Should I Contribute to the Discussion?

Many leaders are unsure about how much they should contribute to the class discussions. Below are several pitfalls to avoid.

1. The leader should remain neutral on a question until the group has had adequate time to discuss it. At the proper time in the discussion the leader can offer his or her opinion. The leader can direct the questions to the group at large, rechanneling those questions that come to him or her.

   At times when the members need to grapple with a question or issue, the most untimely response a leader can make is answering the question. Do not fall into the trap of doing the group members' work for them. Let them struggle with the question.

   However, if the leader has asked the group members to reveal thoughts and feelings, then group members have the right to expect the same of the leader. A leader has no right to ask others to reveal something he or she is unwilling to reveal. A leader can reveal thoughts and feelings, but at the appropriate time.

   The refusal to respond immediately to a question often takes self-discipline. The leader has spent time thinking, reading, and preparing. Thus the leader usually does have a point of view, and waiting for others to respond calls for restraint.

2. Another pitfall is the leader's making a speech or extended comments in expressing an opinion or summarizing what has been said. For example, in an attempt to persuade others, a leader may speak, repeat, or strongly emphasize what someone says concerning a question.

3. Finally, the pitfall of believing the leader must know "the answers" to the questions is always apparent. The leader need not know all the answers. Many questions that should be raised are ultimate and unanswerable; other questions are open-ended; and still others have several answers.

GENESIS TO REVELATION SERIES
REVELATION Leader Guide

Table of Contents

About the Writer

Dr. C. M. Kempton Hewitt served as emeritus professor of biblical interpretation at The Methodist Theological School in Ohio, Delaware, Ohio.

On the Lord's Day I was in the Spirit, and I heard behind me a loud voice like a trumpet. (1:10)

1

IN THE SPIRIT ON THE LORD'S DAY

Revelation 1

DIMENSION ONE: WHAT DOES THE BIBLE SAY?

Answer these questions by reading Revelation 1

1. To whom did God give the revelation? (1:1a)
   God gave the revelation to Jesus Christ.

2. Why was the revelation given? (1:1a)
   The revelation was given to show the servants of God "what must soon take place."

3. How did God make known this revelation given to Jesus Christ? (1:1b)
   God sent an angel to God's servant John.

4. How is John described? (1:2)
   John testifies to "the word of God and the testimony of Jesus Christ."

5. What must those who are blessed do with John's account? (1:3)
   They must read it, hear it, and "take to heart what is written in it."

6. Who is John's message for? (1:4a, 11)

   John's message is for the seven churches in Asia: Ephesus, Smyrna, Pergamum, Thyatira, Sardis, Philadelphia, and Laodicea.

7. Who is described as the one "who is, and who was, and who is to come"? (1:4b, 8)

   John is describing the Lord God.

8. Who else is the message from? (1:4b-5a)

   The message also comes from the seven spirits who are before God's throne and from Jesus Christ.

9. How is Christ described? (1:5a)

   Christ is "the faithful witness, the firstborn from the dead, and the ruler of the kings of the earth."

10. How does John describe himself and his audience? (1:5b-6)

    John and his audience are loved by Jesus Christ, have been freed from their sins by the blood of Jesus Christ, and have been made a kingdom and priests to serve the God and Father of Jesus Christ.

11. What does John say about Jesus Christ being seen again by the world? (1:7)

    John says that "every eye" will see Christ when he returns.

12. Who is speaking in 1:8?

    "The Lord God" speaks in the first person ("I am") and is identified as the Beginning ("Alpha") and the End ("Omega") of all that is.

13. How does John describe himself with reference to the members of the seven churches? (1:9)

    John is their brother and companion. He shares with them "the suffering and kingdom and patient endurance" that are theirs in Jesus.

14. Why was John on Patmos? (1:9)

    John was on Patmos "because of the word of God and the testimony of Jesus."

15. As John describes his experience of being in the Spirit on the Lord's day, what is he told to do? (1:11)

    John is told to write a scroll, describing what he sees, and to send the book to the seven churches of Asia.

16. What are the first things John sees in his vision? (1:12-13)

    As he turns to see the voice speaking to him, John sees seven golden lampstands and in the midst of the lampstands "someone like a son of man."

17. What are the symbolic items of Christ's description? (1:13-16)

    Christ is clothed with a long robe and a golden sash (girdle); his head and hair are white like wool or snow; his eyes are like fire and his feet like gleaming bronze; his voice is "like the sound of rushing waters"; he holds seven stars in his right hand, a double-edged sword is coming from his mouth; his face is like the full strength of the shining sun.

18. What is John's response to this dazzling vision of Christ? (1:17)

    He falls down in fear "as though dead."

19. What two events in the life of Jesus are referred to by Christ in his first speech to John? (1:18b)

    Christ refers to his death on the cross and his resurrection from the dead.

20. As a result of these events, what does Christ possess? (1:18c)

    Christ has "the keys of death and Hades."

21. What does Christ command John to do? (1:19)

    John is to write what he has seen, "what is now and what will take place later."

22. What does Christ tell John about the seven golden lampstands (1:12-13) and the seven stars (1:16)? (1:20)

> *The seven lampstands are the seven churches, the seven stars are the angels of these seven churches.*

DIMENSION TWO:
WHAT DOES THE BIBLE MEAN?

Background. The opening statement places the Book of Revelation in a distinct category in the New Testament: "The revelation [or apocalypse] from Jesus Christ." *Apocalypse* comes from the Greek word *apokalypsis*, meaning "disclosure."

We need to be clear at the outset about how the prophet John understands his apocalyptic encounter. The revelation belongs to Jesus Christ, not to the prophet. God is the source of the revelation to Jesus Christ. In turn, Jesus Christ is the source of the prophet's experience of this revelation.

Many commentaries on Revelation suggest that the central factor in the book is a blueprint of the future, entrusted as a revelation to John. This exact blueprint is then conveyed in the biblical text by means of mysterious codes and symbols. These commentaries suggest that all one has to do is crack the code to know exactly how current events are mirrored in Revelation's text.

This approach has done great harm to Revelation's interpretation. Worse, this approach is really contrary to the belief of Revelation's writer. John's theology teaches that Jesus, the exalted Christ, is the center of faith. Not history. Not the future. Not the evil powers being defeated by "the word of God and the testimony of Jesus Christ" (1:2). But especially, the prophet's experience is not the center of faith. In fact, John is very much an onlooker or observer of the action started by the "Lamb, who was slain" (5:12).

Revelation 1:1-3. John describes himself as "servant." But what he writes is often called *prophecy*. A great deal of scholarly debate continues about Revelation's proper category within the New Testament. Is Revelation an apocalypse only? Is it a prophecy with apocalyptic overtones? Or is Revelation a completely distinct writing with no parallels in or outside of Scripture?

Revelation is certainly apocalyptic. The heightened sense of conflict between the opposing forces of good and evil, the essential pessimism about the possibility of improvements in the here-and-now, the use of animal imagery, the heavy use of numerology and other veiled imagery; all these factors place Revelation clearly in the same class with classical and contemporary apocalyptic writing. But the real home of Revelation is prophecy, as experienced in the early Christian church.

This book grows out of worship and is intended for the use of other Christian prophets ("the angels of the seven churches," 1:20). John almost certainly implies the use of the prophecy in worship. His urgent exhortation to read aloud, listen carefully, understand, and keep the words of this scroll (1:3) tells us a great deal about John's understanding of prophecy. Above all, Revelation is to help the church grow in understanding and obedience. Prophecy tries to help the church understand today's message from the risen Christ, who is the Word of God and who still speaks. Prophecy does not dwell on previous proclamations of Scripture and their interpretations; nor is it interested in the neat categories of past, present, and future. Rather, prophecy tends to run all these together in the immediacy of the moment of the encounter with the living testimony of Jesus.

We are not used to this world of John's prophecy, a strange and admittedly dangerous place in which to live, let alone visit. We like things more orderly, neat, and tidy. Revelation is orderly, but in its own way. For example, John alludes to biblical texts and images on almost every line of Revelation but uses only one direct quotation (15:3). Again, events of the final end of the world are spoken of in the narrative long before we would expect them, if Revelation were an orderly, history-centered work. In some ways, the creative approach of Revelation is more like the collage of a music video than a sequential, logical plan of history. This approach makes Revelation difficult for us to understand. But we make Revelation more difficult only if we try to force it into a mold that it does not fit.

Revelation 1:4-7. Revelation's rich theology about Jesus Christ is one of the most neglected and yet fruitful aspects of the Christian canon. Jesus Christ is described by many titles and actions in this passage. Jesus Christ is "the faithful witness, the firstborn from the dead, and the ruler of the kings of the earth." Jesus Christ has loved us, "freed us from our sins by his blood," and made us to be "a kingdom and priests."

Revelation 1:8. *Alpha* is the first letter of the Greek alphabet, *Omega* the last. John chooses an interesting way of expressing himself when he writes that another revealed name of God is "First and Last." He then expands the name to include time: present, past, and future. If author J. B. Phillips was right, and our God is too small, reflect for a moment on Alpha and Omega as a proper name for God.

Revelation 1:9-20. The participant book points out that audition (hearing as the primary experience) characterizes John's encounter with God. This focus on the sounds of religious experience reminds us that prophecy was probably purely oral in nature. True, John uses words in the text of Revelation to describe his experience; but even this betrays a certain oral character.

The Greek text of Revelation is the most difficult in the New Testament. The technical grammatical studies of the text are quite complex. Many scholars have despaired of understanding or even dealing with the nearly impossible Greek of Revelation. It is as if the experience of hearing and speaking "the testimony of Jesus" (v. 9) cannot be contained by written language.

DIMENSION THREE: WHAT DOES THE BIBLE MEAN TO ME?

Revelation 1

When reading the first chapter of John's prophecy, we could easily concentrate on the fantastic elements of his strange experience. A careful reading of the text, however, shows that John tells little about himself. The main person in the text is Jesus Christ.

The description of such an unusual spiritual encounter raises the question of personal religious experience. The participant book points out that the Book of Revelation is the source of great divisions of opinion. For some Christians, the kind of spirit-induced visions and auditory experiences described by John are not only sought after but considered essential for salvation. For others, the Book of Revelation is discredited because it is based on such experiences. This division of opinion is not simply a contemporary fact; Christians have argued for centuries about Revelation's inclusion in the Bible.

The spiritual challenge of Revelation is to allow its theological and religious value to penetrate our lives. One of the values we are taught by John is the centrality of Jesus Christ. The detail of belief about who Jesus Christ is and what he does for humankind is really quite extraordinary. The eye of the prophet is clearly fixed on Christ, not on the prophet's own mystical experience. Jesus Christ is in control of what is taking place in John's strange experience. Again and again this exaltation and empowering of Christ is affirmed.

In Revelation, John is especially fond of representing Jesus Christ as the great witness. John also writes about "the testimony of Jesus" (v. 9). John makes it clear that Jesus Christ is not only the firstborn from the dead but also the present, living voice of God in the church today.

We may have made Jesus Christ a historical, heavenly reality at the expense of finding ways to allow Jesus Christ to speak in the present. Does Christ speak today? In whose voice do I hear him call? Is his testimony only in words? In whose actions do I see testimony to Christ?

"Be faithful, even to the point of death, and I will give you life as your victor's crown." (2:10c)

SEVEN LETTERS TO SEVEN CHURCHES
Revelation 2–3

DIMENSION ONE: WHAT DOES THE BIBLE SAY?

Answer these questions by reading Revelation 2–3

1. Seven "mini-letters" are sent to seven churches in Asia. Identify the churches. (2:1, 8, 12, 18; 3:1, 7, 14)

   The seven churches are in Ephesus, Smyrna, Pergamum, Thyatira, Sardis, Philadelphia, and Laodicea.

2. In each case, to whom is the letter addressed? (2:1, 8, 12, 18; 3:1, 7, 14)

   Each letter is addressed "to the angel of the church."

3. Which of these seven churches receives no praise? (3:14-22)

   The church in the city of Laodicea is censured, never praised.

4. Which two churches receive only praise and no censure? (2:8-11; 3:7-13)

   The churches in Smyrna and in Philadelphia receive only praise and are not censured.

5. What are some reasons that churches are praised? (2:2, 9, 13, 19; 3:8)

   The churches are praised for perseverance, intolerance of evil persons, endurance in their afflictions and poverty, remaining true to the name of Christ, not denying faith in Christ, love, faith, service, and keeping the word of Christ.

6. Each church receives a promise on the basis of doing what? (2:7, 11, 17, 26; 3:5, 12, 21)
   Each letter ends with a call to be victorious. Those who are victorious (who overcome temptation) will receive a gift from Christ.

7. What are some of the good things promised to those who overcome? (2:7, 11, 17, 26-28; 3:5, 12, 21)
   Those who overcome are promised to eat from the tree of life in paradise; survive the second death; receive the hidden manna; be given a new name on a white stone; be given power over the nations to rule; be given the morning star; be clad in white garments; not be blotted out of the book of life; be acknowledged before God and the angels; be made a pillar in the temple of God to dwell there forever; receive three names: God, the new Jerusalem, and Christ's own name; and receive the privilege of sitting on the throne of Christ with him.

8. Who provides the model of what it means to overcome? (3:21)
   Jesus Christ was victorious (overcame) and was thereby received by God to be seated with God on God's throne.

9. What exhortation closes all the mini-letters? (2:7, 11, 17, 29; 3:6, 13, 22)
   The closing words of each letter are "Whoever has ears, let them hear what the Spirit says to the churches."

10. Who are some of the people censured? (2:2, 6, 9, 14-15, 20; 3:9, 17)
    The censured people include those who call themselves apostles but are not (false apostles), the Nicolaitans, those who call themselves Jews but are not, those who hold the teaching of Balaam, Jezebel and the rich in Laodicea.

11. What are some of the provocative images John uses to describe things Christ censures? (2:4; 3:2-4, 15, 17)
    John uses these images to describe the things Christ censures: forsaking one's first love, sleeping instead of remaining alert, soiling one's garments, being neither hot nor cold but lukewarm, and calling oneself rich and presuming to be self-sufficient.

12. The church at Laodicea is asked to do several things to be acceptable to Christ. What are these things? (3:18-19)

The Christians at Laodicea are called on to buy real gold from God in order to become rich, to wear white clothes to cover their nakedness, to put salve on their eyes so they can see, to be earnest, and to repent.

13. How is Christ described in the opening words of the seven letters? (2:1, 8, 12, 18; 3:1, 7, 14)

- *Christ is the one "who holds the seven stars in his right hand and walks among the seven golden lampstands" (2:1).*

- *Christ is "the First and the Last, who died and came to life again" (2:8).*

- *"Christ has a "sharp, double-edged sword" (2:12).*

- *Christ's "eyes are like blazing fire" and his feet "like burnished bronze" (2:18).*

- *Christ "holds the seven spirits of God and the seven stars" (3:1).*

- *Christ is the holy and true one. He "holds the key of David" and has the authority to open and shut (3:7).*

- *Christ is "the Amen, the faithful and true witness, the ruler of God's creation" (3:14).*

DIMENSION TWO:
WHAT DOES THE BIBLE MEAN?

Background. Revelation 2–3 comprises seven mini-letters to a collection of Christian churches in Asia Minor (present-day Turkey). The churches addressed in these letters formed some kind of logical network for John, but no one knows what the exact connection was. The cities are diverse, clustered in a geographical area either on the western seacoast of Asia or in the watershed of coastal rivers linked with the Aegean Sea. At the time of Revelation they were not yet organized as a single Christian district, as far as we know.

The reference in Revelation is the first knowledge we have, historically, of some of these churches (Smyrna, Pergamum, Thyatira, Sardis, and Philadelphia). Laodicea is mentioned in the letter to the Colossians (2:1-3; 4:13, 15-16). Ephesus is one of the cities Paul visited (Acts 18:19-20:1) and is also associated in early Christian tradition with the apostle John. With such scant information available, we cannot correctly interpret the many oblique references made in these letters, but we have some clues.

While modern archaeological research is yet incomplete in some of these sites, much has already been learned. Many of these cities were enormously wealthy. Ephesus, for example, was a fabulous city at the height of the Roman Empire. Laodicea was a center of cloth and garment production and had a medical school. Pergamum was clearly the most impressive city of all, having been developed according to a master plan of great cunning. Sardis had been the center of Persian culture and political power in Asia Minor before the Romans and was a city of cultural and economic wealth. Philadelphia and Thyatira were modest cities, but both were prosperous and important in their own ways, as centers of production and crafts. Smyrna was an important Roman post and a constant rival of Ephesus for importance, honor, and wealth. All these cities were diverse in population. Ephesus, Smyrna, Pergamum, Philadelphia, Thyatira, and Sardis were known centers of Roman cultic worship. Studies have also established that a significant Jewish population existed in these cities at the time Revelation was written.

These clues suggest four areas of potential conflict that may explain the tone of several of the letters.

1. Pagan worship and constant temptation to compromise Christian standards of conduct would have been everywhere. Life in some of these cities centered on theater, the games, the cult of the Roman Empire, and the daily need to satisfy the whims of countless gods. The cults were doubtless so pervasive as to, for example, make even shopping for food a religious ordeal for the Christian. Nearly all the professions and trade guilds were based on the Roman gods. A person would have had difficulty surviving as a Christian in such a city.

2. As powerful and wealthy cities, many of these locations must have been dazzling. Surrounded by such riches, Christians would have been tempted to place the primary emphasis of their lives on accumulating a part of this wealth.

3. Both Christians and Jews suffered terribly under the Roman rule of the Hellenistic world. Many Roman citizens would have thought of Jews and Christians as being part of one and the same menace, those who refused to worship the gods.

At the time Revelation was written, Christians in all these cities were periodically in danger of losing their lives for confessing their faith and refusing to offer allegiance to Roman gods. The church in Smyrna, a few years after the writing of Revelation, produced the great martyr Polycarp. His story is the first recorded account of a Christian martyr outside the New Testament and one of the most thrilling accounts of Christian courage.

4. Sadly, another reality in many of these cities was the hostile conflict between the Christian church and the Jewish synagogue. References in some of the seven letters to Jews "who say they

are Jews and are not" (2:9) may be explained by this hostility. Christians and Jews lived under periodic attacks of discrimination and abuse in these cities. As noted above, Romans saw them as members of the same family. Indeed, some of the conflict between Christians and Jews had the earmarks of a family feud. This conflict often led to open hostility on both sides. Christians and Jews agreed, however, that the worship of pagan gods was wrong.

This survey of the seven cities, combined with the comments in the participant book, will give you several points for discussing the seven letters. We can well speculate that the early Christians living in these cities were under tremendous pressure. One can imagine that sharply conflicting opinions arose about how Christians ought to respond to these pressures (e.g., "Should we allow our son to be apprenticed to a goldsmith in a guild whose patron is a Roman god?"). Tempers certainly flared, and opinions became entrenched. This period was a great test for the church.

As stands were taken and defended, we can see how one's enemies could be described as "wicked people" (2:2), "a synagogue of Satan" (2:9), those "who hold to the teaching of Balaam" (2:14), or "Jezebel" (2:20). If we could identify the exact nature of the disputes generating this name-calling, we might be surprised. In all likelihood the points were finely drawn. Perhaps these disputes were not unlike issues that have divided the church recently. Many of the same issues were at stake, especially those concerning the degree of compromise allowable between Christian convictions and the dominant culture.

The Unity of the Church. To understand the larger scheme and this collection of mini-letters, we must look at two questions:

1. Why are these particular churches grouped together?
2. Why does John address the angel of each church rather than the church itself?

When Aleksandr Solzhenitsyn published his book *The Gulag Archipelago* (Harper & Row, 1973), the entire world was caught breathless by his searing insight into an evil system of torture and persecution within the Soviet Union. It was not simply his documented, factual account of a bureaucracy of oppression that astounded us. Rather, his artistic conception of Soviet political prisons as an archipelago—a series of "islands" of mental and physical torture joined together in an identifiable mass of oppression—that shocked us. He saw there a unity, a system of persecution.

Solzhenitsyn's description is really quite close to John's vision from Patmos. He sees the seven churches existing as an archipelago of spiritual concern. Like Solzhenitsyn, John's vision unites these churches and reveals to them a system of evil threatening their "victor's crown" (2:10c), which is not clearly perceived by them. The situation of these seven churches changes when the unity of their situation is perceived. An old trick of tyrants is to separate subjected peoples. If evil systems of oppression can be seen for what they are, much of their power is broken. Further, the unity of the church is seen in the risen Lord who "walks among the seven golden lampstands" (2:1) without ceasing.

I can find no other reason for addressing these particular seven churches. Certainly they were not yet organized under ecclesiastical government. Several cities neighboring these, which normally would have been included in a "region of churches," are not mentioned: Colossae, Troas, and Perga, for example. (Colossae was close to Laodicea; Troas and Perga figure prominently in Paul's missionary journeys.)

The second question is equally difficult: Why *angel* and not simply *church* in the first line of each mini-letter? If an archipelago of unity is created by the nurturing presence of the risen Christ, Christ must also have a means to intervene on behalf of these churches. Throughout Revelation, angels carry out the will of God. Each church has its angel. Angels reprove as well as encourage. Angels destroy and angels build in Revelation. Angels are not present in these churches merely to condone and protect. They communicate the reality of the unseen world revealed in the vision portrayed by John. Angels make real the totality of Christ and his church.

Victorious Living. These letters portray a call to a life of victory. The churches are constantly reminded to remain faithful, to continue to resist evil, and to persist in enduring the unendurable. Secular heroism is not what they are asked to follow. Rather, the courage and endurance called for are modeled on the life and example of the One who speaks "the words of him who is the First and the Last, who died and came to life again" (2:8).

Revelation makes great use of the life of Jesus of Nazareth as a living example. Constantly, we find Jesus Christ in both the background and foreground of Revelation, encouraging Christians who are experiencing exactly the same kind of rejection, torture, and death to which he was subject while on earth. Success under persecution, therefore, must have a longer perspective than earthly existence. The presence of angels reminds the hearers of Revelation that another dimension of existence transcends an earthly view. Death here is life "in the paradise of God" (2:7).

While this outlook on Christian existence may appear distant and strange to you, many people today can identify with it. The Book of Revelation has been brought to life again and again in those times and places where suffering for one's confession of Christ is a certainty. As you read this book, remember that somewhere today Christians are devouring Revelation's message with a hunger born of the immediacy of cruel oppression, torture, and the hourly threat of death.

If Revelation seems abnormal to us, maybe what is abnormal is not the book but our easy circumstances. The irony of this condition is, of course, that Revelation seeks to demonstrate to all "who hear it and take to heart what is written in it" (1:3) that an unseen archipelago of evil threatens to destroy the testimony of Jesus Christ, even when the evil is not clearly evident.

DIMENSION THREE: WHAT DOES THE BIBLE MEAN TO ME?

The Challenge to the Seven Churches and Our Challenge: Right Belief and Right Action

We may feel a lack of harmony among these mini-letters. They portray a lean, muscular form of Christianity that is distant from the variety practiced in many of the local churches we know best.

Is it possible to remain sharp and devoted to the call of Christ when persecution is almost unknown? Perhaps we are asking the wrong question, as many prophetic voices in our land are trying to teach us. They identify issues and concerns that are powerful and potentially dangerous for those who get involved.

We are not in such a different position from that of the time of Revelation. Difficult moral decisions face us every day. The consequences of these decisions may be of more import for the future of the world than in the time of John the prophet.

Perhaps the most helpful lesson of Revelation 2–3 is the recognition of Christ's presence in the church as we struggle with the gripping issues of our time. If so, then Christ's voice is still calling to us: Persist by patient endurance in seeking the good and in resisting evil.

The difficulty, of course, is in recognizing the good to be served and the evil to be engaged. The general tone of Revelation also has a lesson for us: it is a labor worthy of the church to work and pray unceasingly to rip the mask from the face of evil.

Make a list of all the people in your community or state or region who, in living memory, have been arrested or charged because of actions motivated by religious beliefs. Include all religious groups, not just Christians. You may be amazed at the length of your list. Analyze the issues involved in the decisions these people made. Even better, interview them. At the end of this project you will have a better appreciation for the seven mini-letters of John.

"Worthy is the Lamb who was slain, / to receive power and wealth and wisdom and strength / and honor and glory and praise!" (5:12b)

WORTHY IS THE LAMB

Revelation 4–5

DIMENSION ONE:
WHAT DOES THE BIBLE SAY?

Answer these questions by reading Revelation 4

1. What did John see and hear? (4:1)

    He saw an open door in heaven and heard a voice like a trumpet calling him to enter the door in heaven.

2. How did John get to heaven? (4:2)

    John was taken to heaven "in the Spirit."

3. How many thrones did John see? (4:2-4)

    John saw twenty-five thrones, one throne on which God was seated and twenty-four more thrones for the elders around the central throne of God.

4. How were the elders dressed? (4:4b)

    "They were dressed in white and had crowns of gold on their heads."

5. Who else is present at this throne scene? (4:5-7)

    The seven spirits of God and the four living creatures are also present.

6. What is the function of the twenty-four elders and the four living creatures? (4:8-11)
    They "give glory, honor and thanks" to God without ceasing.

7. What has God done to be worthy of such praise? (4:11)
    God is worthy because God created all things.

Answer these questions by reading Revelation 5

8. What did John see? (5:1-2, 6)
    John saw, in God's right hand, a scroll sealed with seven seals; a mighty angel shouting; and the Lamb of God.

9. Who is the mighty angel looking for? (5:2)
    The angel searches for someone worthy to break open the seven seals on the scroll.

10. Can anyone open the seals? (5:3)
    Although several evidently have tried, both in heaven and on earth, all have failed.

11. Who finally is found to open the seals? (5:5)
    Jesus Christ, "the Lion of the tribe of Judah, the Root of David," alone is worthy.

12. What does the Lamb do? (5:7)
    The Lamb takes the scroll from the right hand of God.

13. What happens when the Lamb takes the scroll? (5:8-9)
    The twenty-four elders and the four living creatures fall down in worship before the Lamb and begin to sing.

14. In the new song, what is it that makes the Lamb worthy to open the seals? (5:9-10)
    The Lamb has ransomed all humanity by his death and has created a new kingdom and priests to serve God and to rule the world.

15. How many angels respond in praise of the Lamb? (5:11)

"Many angels, numbering thousands upon thousands, and ten thousand times ten thousand"—a countless number—praise the Lamb.

16. Do only the elders and angels sing praise? (5:13-14)

No, all creation, including all creatures, lift their voices to praise the Lamb and God who sits on the throne.

DIMENSION TWO: WHAT DOES THE BIBLE MEAN?

The Book of Revelation often depends on spirits and angels of various lands. Some of the uses to which John puts these unseen beings are quite unusual. We have already met "seven spirits" (3:1, 4:5) and seven angels (1:20). Revelation 4–5 describe the heavenly court of God and the Lamb, giving us a number of helpful insights about these beings.

In Revelation, God and Christ appear as elevated, sovereign figures. They rule and control the direction of the universe. They are concerned about the inhabitants of earth but do not deal with them directly. For example, Christ is present in the churches, but by means of his angels. In Revelation 1:20, the seven angels are symbolized by stars. In Revelation 4:5, the seven spirits are symbolized by blazing lamps. Stars and lamps are sources of light, images for understanding or for revelation. These images make clear that Christ communicates his presence on earth through spirits and angels. The number seven suggests the completeness of this activity.

Christ is everywhere present in his churches and elsewhere on earth. He is represented, and his presence made real, by means of seven spirits. The work of conversion and conviction rests in the hands of these spirits and the angels. But they do not work alone and unaided. Their means of communication is the prophets.

The Book of Revelation is the work of the risen and exalted Christ, who is worshiped with God in heaven. He has brought about this revelation by sending his Spirit to encounter the prophet John. What we see and hear in this book is "of the Spirit," a broad clue to the universal work of the seven spirits and angels at work in our midst. The source of revelation, in other words, is Jesus Christ. But this revealing Christ is also the subject of the Book of Revelation.

Revelation 4:4-8. We are now beginning to meet some of the many symbolic figures of Revelation. Some of these figures will have clear, precise meanings; others will not. Symbolism is complex as an art form. At times it has exact one-to-one meaning, while at other times symbolism works by being plastic and ambiguous. The images of the twenty-four elders and the living creatures in these verses are excellent examples of both kinds of symbolism.

The twenty-four elders are usually seen with the four living creatures and will appear again (Revelation 7:11; 14:3; 19:4). The elders represent the redemption brought about through Christ, the Lamb who was slain. They are twenty-four because the twelve tribes of Israel made up the old covenant and twelve new tribes make up the church. Quite possibly, the new twelve are the twelve apostles of Revelation 21:14, the foundation of the New Jerusalem. We can be fairly certain about this conclusion, since John is so consciously aware of the "old/new" issue. Symbolically, then, John is saying that Christ has redeemed all of history. Redemption cannot be complete unless the reality of Israel is taken into account.

The four living creatures are another matter. They have no precise equivalents in the concrete or historical reality of our existence. They are generally thought to represent creation's totality. These creatures are chosen as the strongest, swiftest, bravest, most intelligent representatives of creation. (Christian tradition has also identified these figures as representative of the four evangelists: Matthew, Mark, Luke, and John.)

Revelation 4:11. God and Jesus Christ are called "worthy" by the massed worshipers. This verse reveals an important idea in John's theology. He believes that we can speak exactly the same way about God and about Christ because complete unity exists between them. This position is distinctive in the New Testament, characteristic only of the books associated with the name *John*. We will find later in Revelation that the key strategy of the evil forces will be to drive a wedge between God and Christ. John cleverly sees that once God and Christ are divided, the possibility of success in deceiving gullible earth dwellers is much greater.

Before the real action of the book begins, then, John is careful to make crystal clear the complete equality and unity of "the Lord God Almighty" and "the Lamb, who was slain."

Revelation 5:1-4. What is written on the scroll? The safest assumption seems to be that it contains the judgments that are about to take place. John's book is a crafted piece of biblical literature. If he had wanted to, he could easily have portrayed Jesus reading from the scroll as the judgments are pronounced. The fact is, John did not use this device, suggesting that what is written on the scroll is not at issue. Rather, the wax seals that keep the scroll from being revealed are the focus of attention.

The scroll comes from the hand of God. Perhaps we are to imagine that at some prior time God wrote on this scroll the divine design for history. Only the Lamb is able to initiate the events soon to break out. The scroll is perfectly sealed (seven seals), therefore, only "perfection" can break the seals.

Revelation 5:5. While these names for Jesus ("the Lion of the tribe of Judah, the Root of David") might sound familiar, they appear nowhere else in the New Testament. Elsewhere, Jesus is "descended from Judah" (Hebrews 7:14) and the "Root of Jesse" (Romans 15:12). Why does John use these names here and now? We have already seen that John finds fulfillment of promises to the twelve tribes of Israel in the redemption of Christ. These distinctive titles for Christ remind readers of Christianity's connection to Judaism. The Lamb is not only of the tribe of Judah; he is also the Lion of Judah. Likewise, he is not only sprung from the root of Jesse (David's father); he is the root of Jesse and David.

These titles fix the Christ as the co-Creator of human history. Without this belief, we might assume that Jesus Christ is subordinate to the twists and turns of history. John pushes the recognition of Christ's predominance further back into history than other New Testament writers. For the prophet John, as for the author of John's Gospel, Christ existed before existence itself.

In a sense, the whole of Revelation pivots on the fact that Christ "triumphed" (5:4) and thus was worthy to open the seven seals. If he had not triumphed, the scroll would remain sealed.

We have already seen in the seven mini-letters a repeated call to overcome (to be "victorious"). This call will be a constant theme in Revelation. At various times, the evil forces of Satan will seek to overcome the faithful. At other times, the people of God will be encouraged to triumph. In Revelation 3:21, the example for the church at Laodicea is Christ's overcoming: "To the one who is victorious, I will give the right to sit with me on my throne, just as I was victorious and sat down with my Father on his throne."

But what has Christ done to overcome? The answer is hinted in the full title of Jesus: "the Lamb, who was slain" (5:6, 12). In death's exaltation, Jesus overcame the powers of Satan. He has presented his victory to God, who sits on the throne, and he is granted a place there with God. The fact that Jesus Christ is accepted by the heavenly court as "worthy" means that God has judged his death victorious. For John, the death of Christ is a glorious victory that must be confirmed by the heavenly court. Put another way, our salvation is based on a heavenly judgment, witnessed by countless hosts.

Revelation 5:8-10. The participant book speaks of the rich liturgical heritage in Revelation. When John speaks about golden bowls of incense as the prayers of God's people, he adds immeasurably to our understanding of prayer. The use of incense as a symbol of prayer is common in the Old and New Testaments. John adds a delightful twist; the language of the text suggests that the saints ("God's people") of earth, not yet present with Christ, are made present by their prayers. This idea makes prayer representational. Usually prayer is thought of as petition. But here John finds the absent saints present by anticipation through their prayers. John describes a remarkable insight, that Christians can "visit" heaven by means of prayer. His account also implies that worship in the heavenly court would be incomplete without the prayers of the saints. How can this be?

In Revelation the heavenly court is influenced several times by the actions of the saints. John thus places great importance on what Christians do and say. His point is exactly this: In the confessions and moral actions of the faithful, the Lamb again and again conquers. His conquest of evil does not depend on the conquest by his people; but his conquest is also not complete until they, too, have triumphed. By the conquest, the Lamb created a new kingdom (5:10); and this kingdom must be filled. The kingdom is not a place; it is people.

The texts of the old songs are, "Holy, holy, holy / is the Lord God Almighty, / who was, and is, and is to come" (4:8); and "You are worthy, our Lord and God, / to receive glory and honor and power, / for you created all things, / and by your will they were created / and have their being" (4:11). Notice that the "old songs" are not out-of-date, old-fashioned, or null and void. Rather, they are completed.

The song to God in 4:11 speaks of creation. This creation includes the formation of a redeemed people. The redemption of Christ has created this kingdom of priests. With Christ's redemption comes the glimmer of the final victory for God's people. This victory has been established as the final outcome since before the foundations of the world. And so, a "new song" is being sung in heaven to glorify Christ and the "kingdom and priests" (5:9-10).

DIMENSION THREE:
WHAT DOES THE BIBLE MEAN TO ME?

Revelation 4

(NOTE: Participant book has questions related to 4:1-8, 9-11.) Group members will be able to describe recent fantasy films and literature that include pictures of existence far more fantastic than this heavenly court scene. Or you may display newspaper or magazine pictures of creatures from these films and stories. The difference is, of course, that John's prophetic description is meant to challenge the suggestion that God is removed and indifferent. The remarkable aspect of Revelation 4–5 is the involvement of the Godhead with our human situation. The scene, as it is played out, sets in motion events that are intended to bring history to the conclusion intended by God from the beginning. This involvement is hardly indifference.

Again, to speak of God as *worthy* is distinctly odd. This word involves an evaluation of God. At first glance, evaluating God might seem inappropriate. What right does the creation (us) have to judge whether God (the Creator) is worthy?

Revelation is very much concerned with the real world of pain, persecution, and suffering. John presents here an implicit recognition that, whether it is right or not, the created order does question God's worthiness. The reader will do well to keep in mind the answer (4:11). Without it we might despair as we read on.

Revelation 5

(NOTE: Participant book has questions related to 5:1-5, 6-14.) The marvelous drama portrayed so vividly by the prophet makes us want to stand and cheer. The events of the day often remind us that, were we totally dependent on our human heroes, we would be in a sad condition. Revelation has a distinctive perception of Jesus Christ. He is seen as a champion among the best heaven, hell, and earth can field. Jesus Christ alone survives the contest.

Perhaps we do not like Jesus to appear competitive. The inner core of truth, however, is that the creature will always try to pull down God, the Creator, from the divine place of honor. The only solution is for the co-Creator, Jesus Christ, to demonstrate that God is God and cannot be put down by angels, creatures of the nether realm, or human agents of evil.

"You are worthy to take the scroll / and to open its seals." (5:9b)

THE BOOK OF THE SEVEN SEALS

Revelation 6–7

DIMENSION ONE: WHAT DOES THE BIBLE SAY?

Answer these questions by reading Revelation 6

1. What happens when the Lamb opens the first seal? (6:1-2)

    One of the four living creatures tells a white horse and its rider to "Come!"

2. What does the rider of the white horse do? (6:2)

    The rider goes out "as a conqueror bent on conquest."

3. What happens when the Lamb opens the second seal? (6:3-4a)

    A second living creature tells a red horse and its rider to "Come!"

4. What happens to the rider of the red horse? (6:4bc)

    God permits the rider "to take peace from the earth," causing violent conflict, symbolized by a "large sword."

5. What happens when the Lamb opens the third seal? (6:5)

    A third living creature tells a black horse and its rider to "Come!"

6. What does the rider of the black horse do? (6:6)

    He weighs out grain at greatly inflated prices, symbolizing scarcity of food.

7. What happens when the Lamb opens the fourth seal? (6:7-8a)
   A fourth living creature tells a pale horse and its rider to "Come!"

8. What does the rider of the pale horse do? (6:8bc)
   He (Death) and Hades are "given power over a fourth of the earth to kill."

9. What did John see when the fifth seal was opened? (6:9-11)
   He saw the martyrs being comforted.

10. What happened when the sixth seal was opened? (6:12-17)
    There was an earthquake, and all the people hid from "the wrath of the Lamb."

Answer these questions by reading Revelation 7

11. What happens at the opening of chapter 7? (7:1)
    An interlude is created by four angels holding the wind from all points of the compass, thus causing a great calm.

12. What takes place in the next scene? (7:2-3)
    A fifth angel brings a seal and, with the help of the other four angels, places a mark on the forehead of Gods servants still on earth.

13. How many of God's servants are sealed, and how is the number determined? (7:4-8)
    Twelve thousand from each of the tribes of Israel are sealed, making a total of 144,000.

14. Where does the next scene take place? (7:9)
    The next scene takes us back to the heavenly court, standing before the throne of God and in front of the Lamb.

15. Who is present that we have not seen before? (7:9)

    A multitude of human beings who have come from all parts and cultures of the globe are standing before the throne.

16. How did this group get to heaven? (7:13-14)

    They "have come out of the great tribulation" to get to heaven.

17. What is given to this great multitude? (7:15-17)

    They are granted satisfaction of all their needs, the task of serving God in the heavenly precincts, the Lamb for their shepherd, the springs of living water to drink, and consolation of all their sorrows.

DIMENSION TWO: WHAT DOES THE BIBLE MEAN?

The Structure of Revelation. With the opening of the seals, we confront the issue of the literary structure of Revelation. Since the time of the earliest theologians, this issue has been argued and has even divided local churches.

The Book of Revelation is not nearly as complex as is the history of its interpretation. Those who have carefully studied the history of Revelation's interpretation have learned to concentrate on the value of Revelation's ideas rather than on its structure. The lives of many people have been severely damaged by means of misguided and compulsive dissection of Revelation. Much of this search was for the hidden "key" of Revelation that would unlock the secrets of the future of the nations.

Revelation 6–7 gives an excellent example of the structural issues in Revelation. We begin with an orderly opening of the seals. But soon interruptions occur. The description of the martyrs at the foot of the heavenly altar (6:9-11) interrupts the opening of the fifth seal. The interlude created by the scene of the 144,000 being sealed (7:1-8) and the description of the multitude in white robes (7:9-17) break the pattern of the sixth (6:12-17) and seventh seals (8:1).

These events are just the beginning of broken patterns. The seventh seal is described in Revelation 8–9. Within the action of the seventh seal, the seven trumpets appear.

Consistent with a pattern of interruptions, Revelation 10:1-11 concerns fresh subjects. Another clear break in Revelation's development occurs in 12:1, which announces the woman clothed with the sun. While all the seals have been broken and all the trumpets sounded by the time we come to 12:1, we find similar material again in Revelation 15:1–19:10. In these chapters we meet seven angels with seven bowls, all of which create more havoc and destruction, punctuated by scenes of heavenly worship.

This collapsing of time—past, present, and future—does not seem to bother John, nor should it bother us. God has saved the people in the past, saves them in the present, and will save them in the future. We are bound to overlook this central, evangelical message of salvation if we are preoccupied with where the great tribulation is located, in reference to the millennium as it relates to the Last Judgment. In the end, these efforts serve only to classify and divide people one from the other, an outcome contrary to the central message of Revelation. That central message is this: Christ is working out the creation of the one people of God, a priestly nation of all peoples of the world, who will join together with the entire created order in the joyful service of the praise of God.

Revelation 6:1-8. John prepared us well in chapters 4 and 5 for this scene. When we left the heavenly court, the Lamb was holding the sealed scroll. He was surrounded by myriads of angels, the four living creatures, and the twenty-four elders. All these personalities will have distinct roles to play in the events that follow.

When John was spiritually transported to the open door of heaven, a voice invited him to "Come" (4:1). The action following the breaking of the first four seals will be initiated in the same way. Voices (this time like thunder, not like a trumpet) summon each of the four horses and its rider with the powerful, bold command "Come!"

The First Seal: The White Horse and Rider (6:1-2). This description is not completely parallel with the three that follow. The rider is armed with a bow, an instrument of war, but no specific destruction is described. The action this rider takes is general: He conquers. We learned in the previous chapter that overcoming (being victorious) is what Jesus as the Lamb has done. Because the Lamb opens the seals, it is unlikely that we are to take the rider of the white horse for Christ. Rather, this rider probably conquers for Christ. The image is military. A reader in the ancient Roman world would understand this figure to symbolize a victorious warrior.

The Second Seal: The Red Horse and Rider (6:3-4). We are not to think that these figures of destruction disturb God's role as Ruler of history. The second horse and rider are given temporary permission by God to keep the peacemaking efforts of nations from succeeding. In Revelation, the peace created by earthly leaders is seen as frail. Political peace is unreliable and can easily lead to war. This idea, also firmly entrenched in the Old Testament prophets, is presented with startling boldness here. The horse and rider do not need to incite war. Peace is broken when the hand of God is withheld. This rider's task is a chilling reminder that all peace comes from God, even the fragile peace of human design. We would be wrong to conclude that it is useless for human beings to try to make peace. Rather, the witness here is to the Source of all peace.

The Third Seal: The Black Horse and Rider (6:5-6). The conditions of famine following the trail of the horse and rider are grotesque. A day's wage (one denarius) will buy only enough grain to permit a scant measure for a small family. We are not told what causes this scarcity, but events in our world today give us insight into the causes of hunger: political chaos and injustice, war, a breakdown in trade, hoarding, and drought. We are to use our imaginations, which is not difficult in an era when millions starve for all the above reasons in every part of the globe.

The Fourth Seal: The Pale Horse and Rider (6:7-8). The worst is saved until the last. This horse is pictured with a rider (Death) and one who follows him (Hades). The color *pale* might better be translated "sickly green," the color of death. Why Death and Hades? Hades is the place of death. One could just as well say "double death" or "death with a vengeance." The death brought by this ghastly pair is caused by armed violence, famine, and plague (disease). Finally, even nature turns on humanity when animals maul and kill people.

The devices of narration are worth following carefully. John's account is peppered with "I heard" or "I looked." He weeps. He counts. He agonizes. He converses with the actors in his vision.

Revelation 6:9-11. *The Fifth Seal.* What causes this violence? Why has God permitted such destruction? Revelation lives and breathes in an atmosphere unlike the rest of the New Testament. In the Gospels, Jesus enters Jerusalem on a donkey, a sign of his peaceful kingdom. Here, he sends out warriors mounted on steeds of war. John and his churches lived in a violent world. Rome was constantly making war on the church. Under this seal, the fifth, we will see that those who have been killed by the sword of Rome cry for vengeance from God for the blood of the Christian martyrs (6:10).

This entire chapter is an example of realism. The world exists by violence. As tragic as this is, it is true. The violence of the world spills over to crush the lives of good people. The Gospels and the book of Revelation argue that injustice will not forever go unpunished. The Bible is clear, however, that justice must be left to God. The careful reader will observe that, in Revelation, God's people who suffer on earth conquer by their faithful witness, not by the sword. The irony of violence in Revelation is that the saints are nonviolent.

The saints who have been martyred for their witness to Christ dwell under God's altar. With this detail, a new piece of equipment is added to the vision of the heavenly court. The altar of God is the place of prayer. The saints are there because their lives of sacrifice are a heavenly imitation of Christ's supreme sacrifice. Their blood cries out for the complete ingathering of all God's people to be with Christ.

This passage gives hope to those who in John's time must yet die a martyr's death. Christ has already said to those in Smyrna, "Be faithful, even to the point of death" (2:10c). This passage has continued to give great comfort to the millions of Christians who have lived in daily fear for their lives through the centuries. Revelation 6:9-11 is one of the few places in the Bible that provides a sustaining image for those who must die by reason of their Christian confession.

Revelation 6:12-17. *The Sixth Seal.* The dangers lurking behind the sixth seal would have been especially believable to John's readers. Some of the cities he was addressing had been destroyed by massive earthquakes, and the people of the geographical area lived in constant fear of them. The heavens were studied intensely, by not only navigators and scientists but also religionists. Many of the cults that form the background to John's warnings about "Satan's so-called deep secrets" (2:24) were based on astrology. These factors make John's writings quite believable. When stars fall from the sky like figs from a tree, when the moon turns blood red and the sun is eclipsed, then the entire basis for finding security in the universe will vanish.

Revelation 7:1-8. John's appreciation for the place of the twelve tribes in the restoration of God's people is taken directly from Ezekiel 48. The idea of sealing the forehead is also from Ezekiel (chap. 9). In the Ezekiel story, the seal protects the righteous from the approaching slaughter. The purpose in Revelation is unclear and seems simply to be a matter of identifying the "servants of our God" (7:3). We are reminded of the promise to the Philadelphians: "I will write on them the name of my God" (Revelation 3:12c).

The tribe of Dan is missing from this list. This omission is due to an obscure tradition that the antichrist of Revelation was to come from the tribe of Dan. (The list in Ezekiel 48 begins with Dan.)

Revelation 7:9-17. This entire section anticipates the final victory of the Lamb and the restoration of heaven and earth. Gradually John builds a more and more complete picture of the heavenly precincts. At first we know only of the throne of God (4:2-3). Then we have an altar introduced (6:9). Now we learn of a temple (7:15). We need not be troubled that, in the new Jerusalem, there is no physical temple "because the Lord God Almighty and the Lamb are its temple" (21:22). John is speaking in artistic images. A further example of this ambiguity is that the Lamb is also a shepherd (7:17). These beautiful word pictures of theological truth should not be damaged by overly zealous scrutiny. Enjoy them for the access they provide us.

The worship of God's court has become more elaborate (7:12). The list of divine attributes is now quite long. Ascribed to God are praise, glory, wisdom, thanks, honor, power, and strength. It is no accident that the prophet John includes *seven* attributes in this list.

As we will learn, the saints who suffer tribulation on earth can conquer only by their testimony. A synonym for *bearing witness* is *praising God*. A particular kind of biblical theology is implicit in the seemingly simple idea of the righteous conquering by their testimony. This understanding of how life works is often at the root of Jesus' teaching. It can lead to a remarkable sense of relief and liberation. In fact, it is quite possible that this understanding is the basic purpose of John's prophecy.

The idea is that the key to living and acting correctly is to recognize the truth of creation. God is ruler of all that exists because all existence was caused by God, who sustains all that is and directs all that will be. Humans are a part of that creation.

When humans attempt to act powerfully, they usurp the place of God. This act is idolatry. To live in harmony with the rest of the created order and with God requires the human creature to ascribe all power and glory to God, by word and by deed. When this is done, all other power finds its rightful perspective; all power other than God's is powerless. Therefore, the best way to defeat the power of evil is to bear witness to the only power of consequence, that of God the Creator. When we witness to God's power, a true sense of power is shared with the human confessor. In this way, the righteous conquer by testimony.

DIMENSION THREE:
WHAT DOES THE BIBLE MEAN TO ME?

Revelation 6–7

(NOTE: Participant book has questions related to 6:1-8, 9-11, 12-16; 7.) Suffering for Christ is a dangerous idea. We know from the biographical and clinical studies of some modern martyrs that death was the compulsive choice of the person, not the glorious result of a heroic life. Every movement includes persons who become attached to it but do not truly care for the cause or values of the movement; they seek only a reasonable excuse for a meaningful death. At times, it would seem that the world is filled with sick minds who are desperately seeking to find a cross upon which they might hang in public view. We must, therefore, be extremely cautious when speaking favorably about the glory of suffering for Christ.

Yet this misuse of Christian suffering must not allow us to neglect careful attention to the thousands of modern saints whose lives are well worth reflection and imitation. Encourage group members to list the names of persons who fit this description. You may want to do it by looking first at well-known, international figures, such as Father Damien, Mother Teresa, and others; moving next to persons such as Martin Luther King Jr.; then to those saints group members have known personally. All these people live selflessly in seeking to witness to justice; to make life better for others; and to relieve the suffering of those who are ill, homeless, in prison, or marginalized.

Then the seven angels who had the seven trumpets prepared to sound them. (8:6)

THE SEVEN TRUMPETS

Revelation 8–9

DIMENSION ONE:
WHAT DOES THE BIBLE SAY?

Answer these questions by reading Revelation 8

1. What takes place when the seventh seal is opened? (8:1)

   "When he [the Lamb] opened the seventh seal, there was silence in heaven for about half an hour."

2. What happens immediately after the silence? (8:2)

   Seven trumpets are given to the seven angels.

3. What two objects does the other angel have? (8:3)

   The angel has a golden censer and is given incense to burn in the censer.

4. What rises and mingles with the smoke of the censer? (8:4)

   The prayers of "all God's people" rise and mingle with the smoke of the censer.

5. What happens when the angel takes fire from the altar and throws it on the earth? (8:5)

   The fire creates a display of thunder, lightning, loud noises, and an earthquake.

6. What is the next series of seven to be introduced? (8:6)

   The seven angels who will blow seven trumpets are introduced next.

7. What happens following the blowing of the first trumpet? (8:7)

   Hail and fire, mixed with blood, fall on the earth, destroying one third of the plants of the earth.

8. What happens when the second trumpet is blown? (8:8-9)

   A great mountain of fire falls into the sea, destroying one third of the life in and on the sea.

9. What happens when the third trumpet is sounded? (8:10-11)

   A falling star named "Wormwood" turns one third of all fresh water bitter, causing human death.

10. What happens when the angel blows the fourth trumpet? (8:12)

    The sun, moon, and stars lose one third of their light, changing greatly the nature of day and night.

11. Does the action of trumpet blowing continue? (8:13)

    No. A brief interlude takes place during which an eagle announces that the next three trumpets will unleash more devastation for humans.

Answer these questions by reading Revelation 9

12. The sounding of the fifth trumpet sets in motion what event? (9:1-3)

    The Abyss is opened, allowing locusts with "power like that of scorpions" to emerge.

13. How are these creatures limited in their torture? (9:4-5a)

    They cannot harm vegetation or those with the seal of God. They cannot kill, but they can torture. The torture can last only five months.

14. How is their terrible work described? (9:5b-6)

    The locusts' torture is "like that of the sting of a scorpion." People seek to die but can only suffer.

15. How does Revelation describe these creatures? (9:7-10)

    They are fantastic creatures bearing no resemblance to any known reality. They look like horses with human faces, gold crowns, women's hair, lion's teeth, "breastplates like breastplates of iron, " and "tails with stingers, like scorpions."

16. Who is their king? (9:11)

    Their king is an evil angel who up until now has been dwelling in the Abyss under lock and key. His name is Destroyer (Abaddon *in Hebrew,* Apollyon *in Greek).*

17. How else are the last three trumpets described? (9:12)

    They are called "woes."

18. What other group of numbers is introduced when the sixth trumpet is blown? (9:13-14)

    A voice from the four horns of God's altar calls to the sixth angel with the trumpet, commanding that the four destroying angels of the Euphrates be released.

19. What do these destroying angels do? (9:15)

    They make war and kill one third of humankind.

20. What are the troops of these angels like? (9:16-19)

    Hordes of the troops appear ("twice ten thousand times ten thousand," or two hundred million). Their appearance is fantastic (horses with heads like lions, spewing fire, smoke and sulfur, tails like snakes).

21. What is the effect of these woes or plagues on those who are not killed? (9:20-21)

    Remarkably enough, the woes do not cause them to repent of their sins: idolatry, murder, sorcery, sexual immorality, and theft.

DIMENSION TWO:
WHAT DOES THE BIBLE MEAN?

Revelation 8:1-5. References to time are frequent in Revelation. Here silence is maintained "for about half an hour" (v. 1). Does this half hour symbolize a definite number of days, weeks, months, or even centuries? The same question may be asked of the "five months" (9:10). In both cases, it is logical to assume that the prophet John did have some actual, temporal equivalent in mind. But what this time period might be is a mystery that died with the prophet. "Half an hour" probably means a short but discernible period.

The vision of John progressively fills out the picture of the heavenly precincts. The picture will continue to be drawn right to the end of the book, in chapter 21, where we get the most elaborate picture of the new heaven and new earth joined as one in the new Jerusalem. Here we learn that the altar (8:3, 5) is something like the altar of burnt offering associated with the temple in Jerusalem. One of the most detailed descriptions of the temple altar is found in Ezekiel 43:13-17. Historians have often depended on this description to reconstruct what the huge sacrificial altar may have been like. Ezekiel clearly describes "horns" on each of the corners of the altar (43:15). These were projections of the stonework. The four corners are important because they form a kind of divine lightning rod between earth and heaven. The blood of sacrifice was sprinkled on these corners (horns) to consecrate the entire altar prior to burning offerings. At the blowing of the sixth trumpet, a voice speaks from each of these horns of God's altar (Revelation 9:13).

Revelation 8:6-12. The destruction described at the blowing of the first four trumpets echoes the account of Creation in Genesis 1.

The destruction of vegetation of the first trumpet recalls the creation of the third day (Genesis 1:9-12) in which the land, the sea, and all vegetation were created. The destruction of the second and third trumpets (when sea and fresh water are contaminated) recalls the creation of the fifth day in which life associated with water was created (Genesis 1:20-22). Finally, the darkening of sun, moon, and stars announced by the fourth trumpet recalls the creation of the first day, day and night and the light to govern both (Genesis 1: 3-5a).

The implication of this literary technique is that, if God can create the world, God can also destroy it. Here the final destruction is hinted at by limiting it to "a third." But if creation is partially destroyed here, it is restored and made new at the conclusion of Revelation. God is never portrayed in the Bible as only a God of destruction.

Several details concerning the description of these various destructions require some explanation:

First Trumpet (8:7). Destruction by hail is an echo of the seventh plague brought upon Egypt through Moses (Exodus 9:22-26). The description in Exodus also mixes hail with fire. Perhaps this description is of a massive thunderstorm complete with lightning and hail.

Second Trumpet (8:8-9). The phrase "something like a huge mountain, all ablaze" is unclear and reminds us that John is reporting a vision. He is often at a loss to find adequate comparisons from his own experience. The description here probably means a monumental molten object that destroys the water of one third of the seas.

The precise point of "turned into blood" also is unclear. Maybe the color of the sea changed to red. Or perhaps the sea became "red hot." This heating of the water would explain why ships on the sea were destroyed, along with the sea life.

Third Trumpet (8:10-11). The great star falling from heaven is an evil angel, as in 9:1. *Wormwood* is the name of this angel. Revelation frequently makes destruction personal, and this is an example. Wormwood is mentioned elsewhere in the Bible (Proverbs 5:4; Jeremiah 9:15; Amos 5:7). It is a known plant in Palestine that will turn water bitter, if not actually poisonous.

Fourth Trumpet (8:12). To be precise, it should be noted that the lights of day and night shine for only two thirds of the normal time. It does not mean that they shone one-third less brightly.

Notice that the result of the seven bowls of wrath poured out in Revelation 16 is, in part, quite similar to the destruction of the first four trumpets.

Revelation 8:13. The narrative is interrupted at 8:13 to help the reader understand that the first four trumpets are of one kind of destruction and the next three will be of a quite different kind.

Eagles figure prominently in both Ezekiel and Revelation. Recall the four living creatures described in Revelation 4:6b-8, one of which is "like a flying eagle." Ezekiel 17 is an extensive prophetic parable about "a great eagle." (Your preparation for teaching this lesson would be enhanced by reading Ezekiel 17.)

The repeated warning—"Woe! Woe! Woe"—is not simply for emphasis. The next three trumpets are all called "woes" (9:12; 11:14). The prophet keeps count of the woes, possibly because of the break between the second and third woes in Revelation 10–11. (The first, second, and third woes are equivalent to the fifth, sixth, and seventh trumpets.)

Revelation 9:1-11. *The Fifth Trumpet.* The narrative depends on two ideas described more fully elsewhere in Revelation: (1) an angel opening the Abyss is more explicitly and graphically described in Revelation 20:1-3; and (2) the people of God who are not to be harmed have already been introduced in Revelation 7:1-8. This hole may be the same as hell; it is conceived of as a place of chaotic evil that is covered and contained by a lid which is locked with a key.

The description of the locusts (demonic beings) does not mean to suggest they look like any particular known animal. These creatures sting like scorpions; are as big as horses; have long, wavy hair and long, sharp teeth; and are frightfully noisy. The comparison with locusts might include any or all of these points: they move as on wings, they devour at an incredible rate, move in swarms, and have many legs and/or wings. (The Middle Eastern species of locusts have six legs and four wings.) We need only recall numerous descriptions given by primitive people of their first experience of an airplane or train to realize how difficult and dangerous it is to make too much out of the details of the description here.

The five months is a mystery (9:5, 10). It certainly means a period of considerable length. The visitation is not momentary. In this sense, these demonic creatures are not like locusts, which come and go swiftly.

Revelation 9:13-19. *The Sixth Trumpet.* The language of 9:14 might easily be confused. Four angels have not been bound or restrained at the river Euphrates. Rather, as in the case of the four winds being personalized as four angels in Revelation 7:1, these four angels are restraining the cavalry. This is expressed in a kind of shorthand. Revelation 9:15 suggests that these two hundred million cavalry troops are under the control of these four angels. The number is not meant to be taken literally but to convey the sense of an army larger than any before seen.

The command from the four corners of the altar is evidently what determines the number of angel-commanders, but the number could also be explained as representing the four points of the compass.

The "three plagues" (9:18) are a bit difficult to make out. There do not appear to be three different destructions described, but rather, one great machine of death. The three plagues probably refer to the "fire, smoke and sulfur that came out of their mouths."

John gives a fantastic description of the chaos and death created by marauding troops. The result is clear ("a third of mankind" is killed), but the means is not. Because the territory beyond the Euphrates held the dreaded enemies of both Israel and Rome, we are encouraged to conclude that this description is of especially frightening, bloodthirsty human troops. However, the description, especially of the horses (9:17-19), also recalls and echoes that of the demonic locusts of the fifth trumpet (9:7-10).

Revelation 9:20-21. The sin of idolatry is on John's mind and is described here in much greater detail than the other sins. This sin is also reflected in the seven "mini-letters" to the Asian churches (chaps. 2–3). We know from history and archaeology that the worship of many gods was a major preoccupation of the Roman world. The description given here of idolatry, however, has a genuine flavor of the Old Testament (Psalms 115:4- 7; 135:15-17).

The word translated *sexual immorality* probably is meant to cover a range of ritual sexual practices of various Roman cults. This area of concern is related to idolatry.

A wide range of practices are grouped under the sin of "magic arts." The Greek word used means "poison," in the sense of "magic potion." The use of magic is, therefore, virtually the same as idolatry.

DIMENSION THREE: WHAT DOES THE BIBLE MEAN TO ME?

Revelation 8–9

The participant book suggests to center reflection and discussion on the portrayal of God's judgment in Revelation. It is easy to adopt the generalization that Revelation is distinctive in its view of God and of the judgment that God brings on the world. Revelation is the only book of its kind in the New Testament. However, each of the Synoptic Gospels (Matthew, Mark, and Luke) contains at least one chapter called a "little apocalypse," a chapter that contains material similar (and even at times identical) to that in Revelation (Matthew 24; Mark 13; Luke 21).

The God of Revelation is not vindictive or cruel. Rather, Revelation is different from other parts of the New Testament because it portrays, in detail, the nature of God's justice when it confronts unrepentant evil. In Revelation, God does freely grant grace to those who repent of evil. The truth of this good news is seen in the constant references to "God's people" who are redeemed by the blood of the Lamb. Revelation 8–9 has none of this grace to balance a sickening portrayal of the partial destruction of creation. If group discussion leads to comments about the shock of finding God to be this kind of God, you may want to discuss this information.

Many Christians struggle with understanding and accepting a God of both grace and judgment. Our culture does not aid in this understanding, as it does not acknowledge much divine judgment of unrepentant sins. Important to remember is that judgment belongs to God, not to us. We must be careful in how we speak about the sins of others. Otherwise, the sin may actually lie in our judgments and charges against them. In Revelation 9:20-21, the prophet John bases the judgment he has just witnessed squarely on laws taken from the Ten Commandments. Therefore, his judgment of sin is based solidly on the witness of Scripture. Further, he has been a witness to these things and is not basing his conclusions on hearsay or rumor.

The participant book also suggests using the collective imagination of group members in identifying events of human origin and nature which are like the partial destructions narrated in these two chapters. You may be amazed at how many of these you will discover. (The list may include the "El Niño" phenomenon, the phenomena of acid rain and destruction of the ozone layer, biological warfare, cluster bombs and napalm, and so on.)

Since the writing of Revelation, entire populations have been injured or maimed by events in nature and at the hands of humans. At times, this destruction has exceeded Revelation's "a third" of the population. Wars and political cruelty have, in our times, created conditions far worse than some of those described in these two chapters of Revelation. Natural disasters have completely obliterated communities, sometimes leaving nothing in their wake. How are we to view these things? Are they the result of God's judgment? Can we really say God has sent such disasters to earth? Or are they evidence of exactly the same sins spoken of in Revelation 9:20-21: theft, immorality, murder, and idolatry? Are those punished the ones who have committed such sins?

The participant book also raises the possibility of identifying "locked lids over hell." A good example might be nuclear instruments of war. Have we left the lid off an Abyss of pain and suffering by permitting our nation to arm itself with nuclear weapons, by assumed privilege of the dominant class, by failing to address injustice? These or other issues seem perfect to illustrate the relevance of the concept as well as the description of the possible result.

"You must prophesy again about many peoples, nations, languages and kings." (10:11)

A SCROLL BOTH BITTER AND SWEET

Revelation 10–11

DIMENSION ONE: WHAT DOES THE BIBLE SAY?

Answer these questions by reading Revelation 10

1. How is the "mighty angel" of John's vision described? (10:1)
   The angel is "robed in a cloud, with a rainbow above his head; his face was like the sun, and his legs were like fiery pillars."

2. What is the angel holding? (10:2a)
   He has an open scroll in his hand.

3. Where is the angel standing? (10:2b)
   He spans earth and sea, with one foot on each place.

4. After John hears the seven thunders, he is told by another voice not to do what? (10:4).
   He is told not to write down what he has heard the thunders say.

5. What has the "mighty angel" come to do in John's presence? (10:5-6)
   The angel takes a vow that what he says is true: "There will be no more delay!"

6. What will happen, according to this angel, when the seventh trumpet is sounded? (10:7)
   "The mystery of God will be accomplished."

7. What is John instructed to do with the scroll? (10:9)

He is told to take the scroll from the angel and to eat the scroll.

8. What happens when John eats the scroll? (10:10)

John discovers that the scroll is sweet to eat but bitter to digest.

9. What is John told this action means? (10:11)

John must again prophesy concerning many peoples and their leaders.

Answer these questions by reading Revelation 11

10. What is John told to do in this vision? (11:1)

Using a measuring device, he is to measure "the temple of God."

11. How long will "the Gentiles" be permitted to "trample on the holy city" of Jerusalem? (11:2)

They will have "42 months" there.

12. Who is given power to "prophesy for 1,260 days" in sackcloth? (11:3)

God's "two witnesses" are given the power to prophesy.

13. How else are these two witnesses described? (11:4, 10)

They are also called "'the two olive trees," "two lampstands," and "two prophets."

14. What kinds of things are the witnesses given power to do? (11:5-6)

They can defend themselves from harm by a consuming fire that issues from their mouths; they can cause rain to cease, creating droughts; and they can cause plagues of whatever kind they choose.

15. What happens when their testimony is finished? (11:7-8)

They will be killed by the beast from the Abyss, and their bodies will be cast into the streets of Jerusalem ("figuratively called Sodom and Egypt").

16. What happens to their bodies? (11:9-10)

    For "three and a half days" they will be exposed to the taunts of the rejoicing people who observe them.

17. What happens later to the bodies of the two prophets? (11:11-12)

    The prophets will be raised from the dead by the breath of God and called to heaven.

18. What follows this remarkable event? (11:13)

    A great earthquake destroys a tenth of the city of Jerusalem and its people.

19. Are the people of earth affected by the blowing of the seventh trumpet? (11:15-19)

    There is no immediate impact on earth; the scene concerns events in heaven.

20. What do the elders thank God for in their hymn of praise? (11:17-18)

    They thank God for taking power and beginning to reign, rewarding the prophets, and destroying those who destroy God's creation.

21. What new object in the heavenly precincts is introduced? (11:19)

    John sees the ark of the covenant.

DIMENSION TWO: WHAT DOES THE BIBLE MEAN?

Revelation 10:2a, 8-11. The action of this chapter centers on the small, open scroll. This scroll appears first in the hand of a "mighty angel" (10:1) and then is eaten by the prophet John. The entire scene is parallel to Revelation 5, in which another "mighty angel" (5:2) introduces the sealed scroll.

While the little scroll scene of chapter 10 occurs about midpoint in Revelation, it has the character of an initial vision in which the prophet receives his call and is charged with his task. Such a vision is also seen in Ezekiel 2:8–3:3, but there are significant, probably intentional, differences. Ezekiel is not sent to speak to foreign people but only to the house of Israel (Ezekiel 3:5). The rebellious nature of his own people makes Ezekiel's task bitter. In the case of John, the bitterness is in the task of speaking his prophecy to "many peoples, nations, languages and kings" (Revelation 10:11). One of these nations—Rome—is killing God's people, both Jews and Christians, by the thousands.

Conveying a message by means of making the prophet act it out is typical of the prophetic tradition. Such events are sometimes called *sign-acts* because the prophet symbolizes a message by acting out a scene. In this rather strange street theater, God is the divine playwright and director. The prophet is a one-person repertory company.

Jeremiah and Ezekiel were often called to act out signs of prophecy. Perhaps the best known is Jeremiah's construction and wearing of a yoke to symbolize the desire of the Lord that Judah submit to the will of Babylon and its king, Nebuchadnezzar (see Jeremiah 27).

Prophets are considered by most to be divine fools. In the ancient world, the link between such bizarre behavior and holiness was more obvious than it is for us. An honored place in Scripture is kept for those who are willing to appear as fools in the course of being obedient to a divine mandate.

Revelation 10:3-7. The participant book suggests that the "seven thunders" is a kind of polite and poetic way of speaking about God. This image for God's voice is frequent in Scripture (e.g., Deuteronomy 5:22; Psalm 29:3-9), sometimes quite literally suggesting that thunder is God speaking (John 12:28-29).

Revelation 10:4 is potentially confusing. Since we have already seen a sealed scroll (5:1), the casual reader might assume that the angel is being commanded to seal up the open scroll. This is not the case. The order to "seal up" means "do not write," as stated in the rest of the sentence. Scholars have puzzled for centuries over this order. I can find two logical reasons, in addition to those suggested in the participant book, for the prophet not being permitted to write what God had spoken:

1. In contrast with reports of the Old Testament prophets, Revelation never portrays God as speaking directly with humans. On many occasions, a voice or voices "from heaven" speak. But the words of these voices represent a general heavenly mandate. Because Revelation is seriously concerned about the contamination of idolatrous Roman cults (9:20), it is not surprising that John would be reluctant to describe a humanlike God who can be easily contained by a literal quotation. The God of Revelation must remain sovereign in every sense.

2. The bulk of Revelation 12–14 likely is meant to convey, by means of narrative action, the content of the little scroll. Therefore, in the drama of this narrative, it is better to have the prophet wait and witness the content firsthand than to write it down now. This, of course, lends a kind of urgency and drama to the action.

We have no other example in Scripture of an angel swearing an oath. The Old Testament presents a great deal of vow- and oath-swearing; the New Testament tells of much less. Jesus prohibits swearing at all in Matthew 5:33- 37, a passage without parallel in the other Gospels. If John knows of this prohibition, it does not seem to bother him here. The swearing is for effect and lends itself, with several other devices of this chapter, to creating a sense of the significance of the moment. Something serious is about to take place! Taking an oath and raising one's hand are virtually synonymous (Daniel 12:7).

The content of the oath is that there will be no more delay. What will not be delayed is further defined only as "the mystery of God" (10:7). While mysteries and secrets figure highly in Revelation, the use here is singular and quite unique. We are reminded that Jesus told his disciples that they had been entrusted with the secret (mystery) of the kingdom of God (Mark 4:10-12). The key word, in both Mark and in Revelation 10:7, is the Greek word *musterion*, often translated "secret," but here correctly translated as "mystery."

In the rest of the New Testament, Christ is God's mystery personified (see Colossians 2:2). We could well capture the meaning here into a paraphrase: "The kingdom of Christ in all its fullness will not be delayed." This is the essence of the message given by the "mighty angel." This interpretation is strengthened when one recognizes that, in the Gospels, the term *delay* is a technical one, always connected with the return of Christ in power. Christians are constantly warned not to grow lax during the delay of Christ's coming.

Notice too, how this mystery is characterized. God has consistently announced through the ages that the mystery of God's kingdom will be fulfilled. The history of the prophets is the history of God's mystery of salvation. An exciting moment has come for the prophet John, for soon he will witness personally the drama of this mystery unfolding with the sights and sounds of heaven.

Revelation 10:8-11. Why does this story about the prophet's call come here, rather than earlier? In part, the answer is clear only when Revelation 10 and 11 are viewed together. As we will see, the drama of the two martyred prophets in Revelation 11:1-13 is a kind of synopsis of prophet ministry from Moses until the time of John, the prophet of Patmos. This perspective causes us to pause to recognize the role of prophecy suggested by Revelation.

The fundamental role of the prophet is to give guidance to the people of God. Also, prophecy is most at home in oral discourse. The immediacy of speech in a particular situation with a particular people makes prophecy what it is. The oral nature of prophecy is why the concept of testimony/witness is so crucial to the thought of Revelation (11:3, 7). *Testimony* is confession with the tongue; *martyrdom* is confession with one's life. The prophet testifies because Jesus testified. Both bear witness to the truth of God. But Revelation goes even further. Testimony is possible for the prophet because it is participation in "the testimony of Jesus" (1:2).

We have seen consistently that John's remarkable auditory and visual experience is not for his private benefit or enjoyment. Prophecy is intended to help people understand God's will for the present. When the message is announced, however, it is often misunderstood. Even when the message is understood, it is usually rejected by the majority of those for whom it is intended. Again and again, from Moses to John, the prophets were rejected, beaten, punished, exiled, and ridiculed. The work of the prophet has a bitter core. No wonder prophets of the Old Testament often resisted their vocation!

Revelation's viewpoint is that just as Jesus remained faithful and triumphed by his testimony to the truth so also the prophets can remain faithful and triumph if they, too, testify in a way consistent with the witness of Jesus Christ. The Greek word for *testimony* is *marturia*; the word for *martyr* is *martus*. This obvious, intimate connection makes the point of Revelation eloquently. The final testimony of Jesus was surrender to a martyr's death. The final witness of the representative two prophets in Revelation 11:1-13 is martyrdom in the same city "where also their Lord was crucified" (11:8).

We have already seen the high honor given the masses of martyrs in Revelation (6:9-11). How does this help the Christians of the Asian churches who are suffering daily and expecting their own deaths? Indeed, how does it help today's Christians who are in the same circumstance? Revelation gives an answer. This answer is not limited to the hope that the day of final judgment will no longer be delayed, although this is certainly basic to the apocalyptic viewpoint of Revelation. Much of Revelation is concerned with how Christians are victorious in their persistence and faithfulness in the interim, before the final judgment of God. The answer to victorious survival is to live the life of "the testimony of Jesus" and his prophets of all ages.

Eating the scroll is an image for internalizing the good news of Christ and his kingdom. Taking in the good news comes prior to speaking ("You must prophesy again," 10:11).

What is spoken? Above all, this is modeled in the many scenes of worship around God's throne. Christians survive by the praise of God in liturgy, music, prayer, and testimony. The vision that generated the Book of Revelation came to John while he was in the Spirit on the Lord's day (1:10).

No other New Testament book provides such a remarkable rationale for the necessity of well-ordered worship. Liturgy, in the eyes of Revelation, is necessary for Christian survival. Countless case studies in church history uphold this conviction. For instance, Sunday morning worship has kept alive the aspirations and courage of the black community in the United States and in South Africa. Only those who have not lived under inhuman conditions might struggle to understand this biblical principle.

There is more. Since the entire book of Revelation is John's vision of the testimony of Jesus, we must not miss the forest for the trees. The circumstance of the first readers of Revelation was of powerful, destructive political forces at work in the Roman Empire of the first century. We may be tempted to accept the categories of earthly powers in the attempt to understand our circumstances. Revelation will not let us do this. This vision invites hearers to engage other, more powerful, but unseen realities in assessing their circumstances.

The powerful images of Revelation are an invitation to Christians to use their imaginations—sanctified by the concept of the "Sovereign Lord, holy and true" (6:10)—in rethinking their situations. Armed with this witness, that which may at first appear overwhelming may be seen for what it is: crippled, desperate, frightened, and powerless. This remarkable perspective is precisely the point of the interview between Pilate and Jesus:

[Pilate] went back inside the palace, "Where do you come from?" he asked Jesus, but Jesus gave him no answer. "Do you refuse to speak to me?" Pilate said. "Don't you realize I have power either to free you or to crucify you?" Jesus answered, "You would have no power over me if it were not given to you from above." (John 19:9-11a)

Revelation 11:1-3. The temple of God mentioned is the Jerusalem temple known to Jesus. This temple had been trampled over (11:2) by the Roman legions of Titus in AD 70. The destruction and looting of the temple was a traumatic event for Christians as well as Jews.

For the Jewish Palestinian community, this event accelerated the development of rabbinical forms, institutions, and practices. Judaism has not seen a return to a priestly cult and a system of sacrificial worship since AD 70.

For Christianity, the devastation of Jerusalem and its temple also created a crisis, since the "mother church" of Christianity was in Jerusalem and was associated with the Jewish-Christian pillars of the apostolic era. Western Christians may have a difficult time understanding this crisis feeling; but for Christians of the Pauline church, Christianity without a center in Jerusalem would have been difficult to conceive. This fact is reflected in various passages of the Synoptic Gospels, where the destruction of the temple is viewed as evidence that the return of Christ in judgment cannot be far off (Mark 13:1-2, 14-22).

The reason for not including the Court of the Gentiles in this protection is difficult to explain. Certainly it must have something to do with excluding those who have not remained faithful to Jesus Christ. Ironically, the Court of the Gentiles is the only remaining part of the temple precincts. The western wall of the Herodian Temple formed one of the boundaries of the Gentile court. This wall can be seen in Jerusalem today.

Revelation 11:4. Olive trees, as cultivated in Palestine, are noted for their strength, age, and dependability. Thus these trees are a frequent biblical image for blessings bestowed by God. Oil from the trees is essential to Palestinian life. A measure of their importance is the command given by God regarding holy war. While humans and beasts were to be put to death utterly, Israel was strictly prohibited from cutting down fruit trees (Deuteronomy 20:19-20). These trees would have been primarily olive trees.

The lampstands may represent the entire church as enlightened by the prophetic ministry of John and others like him. The connection may seem remote, but the idea is essential to understanding Revelation. In essence, the affirmation suggests that without prophecy the church cannot be a light in the world.

Revelation 11:5-6. Is it credible that prophets could have such power? A careful reading of the Old Testament narrative history of Israel will confirm the claim made here. Quite literally, prophets caused nations to rise and fall. (We may also remember that Martin Luther King Jr. created an entire epoch in American history through prophetic leadership.) Of course, personal power was not at stake. Rather, the prophet's commission to speak the word of the Lord was at issue. The call and the message of the prophet create the power. Often prophets resist their commission, pointing to their human frailty. Moses pleaded his lack of eloquence (Exodus 4:10), Jeremiah his youth (Jeremiah 1:6), and Isaiah his sinfulness (Isaiah 6:5). The message between the lines is easy to miss: John wants his oppressed and seemingly powerless listeners to see the depth of the power that lies in "the testimony of Jesus" (Revelation 1:2).

Revelation 11:7-13. Jerusalem was the site of both divine revelation and the attempt to snuff out the source of that revelation, the prophets. In this sense Jesus is the great prophet. The Gospels are careful not to limit Jesus to a prophet's role, because he is more than a prophet. Jesus is the fulfillment of the law and the prophets (Matthew 5:17). Still, he is part of the prophetic tradition and suffers the prophet's normal fate: exile and death.

In this passage the connection between the two prophets and Jesus is so clear as to be unmistakable. The effect is to unite the guild of prophets with Jesus. Even the resurrection and ascension of the two prophets are modeled after Jesus (Acts 1:9). John will soon hear that "the Spirit of prophecy bears testimony to Jesus" (Revelation 19:10d). In chapter 11, we see how this is precisely the case: prophets then and now, says John, destroy evil with their testimony; but they are also tormented, killed, and raised from the dead. We see in these prophets the life of Jesus, the great Prophet.

Revelation 11:17-18. This hymn of praise is weighted heavily with Revelation's faith. The basis of hope for a victorious outcome is, throughout the book, the absolute sovereignty of God. God has power over creation and exists before time and space.

Two phrases need explaining because of the complexity of the poetry in verse 18:

(a) "The nations were angry, / and your wrath has come" pivots on a play on words in Greek. A paraphrase to make the meaning clear might be, "The pagan peoples were filled with wrath, but the moment has come for your wrath."

(b) "The time has come for judging the dead" is meant to be positive hope for the faithful, since the resurrection of the dead is implied in the lines following. The logical connection is that the righteous will be vindicated at the general resurrection.

Notice that this magnificent hymn is a fitting poetic prayer such as might be found in liturgies for the Lord's Supper. The song begins with the word of thanksgiving appropriate to such prayers: "We give thanks to you, Lord God Almighty" (v. 17).

Revelation 11:19. This chapter begins with a vision of the earthly temple in Jerusalem and ends with a vision of the heavenly temple. This vision is a subtle reminder that while the temple in Jerusalem lies in ruins, inhabited by the pagan Roman legions, the temple of God is still intact. God is still in control of life, even though earthly realities might suggest otherwise.

The ark of the covenant in the Old Testament was the item that most clearly conveyed the sense of God's presence. In the temple, the ark resided in the Holy of Holies. At the time of Revelation's writing, the ark was no longer in the Jerusalem temple. The reminder that the ark is still in the heavenly temple is a powerful metaphor for the claim that God has not abandoned the people of God. The description of power surrounding the ark leaves no doubt that God is present in power.

DIMENSION THREE: WHAT DOES THE BIBLE MEAN TO ME?

Revelation 10

The participant book poses questions for discussion about the bittersweet nature of life's most important tasks and experiences. Discuss the responses participants had to these questions. What life experiences have been both bitter and sweet?

The biographies of those persons who have made significant contributions to the church and society invariably speak about experiences of conflict. They tell of proposing changes that are stubbornly resisted by others. This resistance has been true in the history of the antislavery movement, in the women's liberation movement, and in the growing pursuit of equality for a variety of minority groups. All these movements have depended on countless women and men who sacrificed themselves for a cause essential to human welfare and dignity. Some end their experiences in bitterness, some in despair. Most recall something sweet about their involvement.

Not all social reform movements are of equal worth, but most fair-minded people admire the courage and commitment of those who care enough to try to change things for the better. Those who do get involved always find it a bittersweet experience. Events and conflict in our congregational life can also be bittersweet. Perhaps in your congregation, as in many congregations, local church leaders face overwhelming challenges and decisions. How are we to be faithful to this text in these circumstances? Certainly one aspect concerns recognition that actions are never purely "sweet as honey" (vv. 9-10). John's experience suggests that *sourness* (the bitterness of conflict, suffering, opposition, misunderstanding, and so on) is almost always part of the most important actions taken in life.

Revelation 11

The subject of modern prophets is an important one to consider. Very likely, given past history, prophets are all around us today who, if listened to, could lead us to a better understanding of our circumstance, enlighten the factors on which we must base individual and group experiences, and give us the courage of our convictions. The fact is, of course, that we are also surrounded by false prophets. Most of us are reluctant to make judgments about these matters, as well we should be.

Often the true prophets have been branded false and killed or otherwise silenced. Martin Luther King Jr. fit all the criteria of a modern prophet. At the height of his leadership, however, many Christians and others judged him to be unfit to listen to, let alone to follow.

The people of God must always face the agonizing problem of distinguishing between true and false prophets. In part, our response to the claims of prophets must be based on the examples of Revelation. This book places God and the witness of Jesus Christ at the center of its claims. John proclaims a gospel of redemption consistent with the rest of the New Testament and teaches no new doctrine. Further, he makes no claim for himself and his authority other than servant and prophet. John's only mission is to convince hearers that the vision of triumph he has witnessed is from God. These same criteria can be usefully applied today to those persons whom some would call *prophets*.

This calls for patient endurance and faithfulness on the part of God's people. (13:10c)

7

THE WOMAN CLOTHED WITH THE SUN

Revelation 12–13

DIMENSION ONE: WHAT DOES THE BIBLE SAY?

Answer these questions by reading Revelation 12

1. What is the first sign seen by John? (12:1)
   John first sees the "woman clothed with the sun, with the moon under her feet and a crown of twelve stars on her head."

2. What is the woman's condition? (12:2)
   She is pregnant and very close to giving birth.

3. What is the second sign John sees? (12:3)
   John next sees a huge, red dragon with seven heads, each crowned, and ten horns.

4. What does the dragon want to do? (12:4b)
   The dragon waits for the woman to give birth so he can kill the child.

5. What happens to the child? (12:5)
   When the child is born, he is taken up to be with God.

6. What happens to the woman clothed with the sun? (12:6)
   She runs to the desert where she is cared for.

7. What does John describe next? (12:7-9)

John describes a great battle in heaven between "the great dragon" Satan and his angels and Michael and his angels. The outcome is that Satan and his forces are defeated and thrown out of heaven to earth.

8. What are the good news and the bad news resulting from this event? (12:10-12)

The good news is that while Satan is out of heaven, he can no longer make trouble there for Christians. The bad news is that Satan can now do great damage on earth.

9. When the story of the dragon and the woman clothed with the sun resumes, what new information are we given? (12:13-16)

We learn how she escaped. She was given wings to fly into the desert. When the dragon tries to destroy her by flooding the land, the earth itself comes to her aid by absorbing all the water of the flood.

10. How does the dragon respond to this failure? (12:17)

He is so angry that he makes war on the rest of the woman's children, "those who keep God's commands and hold fast their testimony about Jesus."

Answer these questions by reading Revelation 13

11. How is the "beast coming out of the sea" different from the dragon? (13:1)

The beast has crowns on its horns rather than on its head as the dragon does.

12. What is the relationship between the dragon and this beast? (13:2b)

This beast is given the "power and . . . great authority" of the dragon.

13. Which part of this new beast does John carefully describe? (13:3a)

John carefully describes one of the beast's heads, which had been wounded but has healed.

14. How do human beings on earth respond to the beast? (13:3b-4)

They are astonished at the beast and worship it.

15. What does this beast do and for how long? (13:5-7)

The beast blasphemes God and those who dwell in heaven with God. It engages the saints of earth in war, defeats them, and rules over the entire inhabited world for forty-two months.

16. Who succeeds in not being taken in by the beast? (13:8)

Those who have had their names written in the book of life are able to stand against the beast.

17. How are the hearers asked to respond? (13:9-10)

John asks the hearers to listen carefully and to exercise endurance and faithfulness.

18. What appears next? (13:11)

Another beast appears; it looks like a lamb (with two horns) but sounds like a dragon.

19. What is this beast's relationship to the beast described earlier in this chapter? (13:12)

The second beast takes the place of the first beast, has all its authority, but seeks to make the earth's inhabitants worship the first beast, not itself.

20. What methods does the second beast use? (13:13-17)

This beast uses many methods but primarily deceit. The beast performs magical tricks with fire; it creates an image of the first beast that speaks and controls commerce by marking those who agree to worship the beast. The beast places on the hand or forehead a number that lets people buy and sell.

21. What is the number of the beast? (13:18)

The number of the beast is "666."

DIMENSION TWO: WHAT DOES THE BIBLE MEAN?

Revelation 12:1. The "woman clothed with the sun" is one of the most cherished symbols of Christianity. Volumes have been written about the meaning of this vision. A large part of the

Christian church believes that this woman represents the Virgin Mary. While the interpretation is attractive, it does not fit well the story narrated in Revelation 12.

Our limited knowledge of the birth of Jesus and the events following do not conform well to the heavy theme of persecution here. The viewpoint of the Gospels would suggest that Mary was a continuing presence in the life of the mature Jesus. She may have been with Jesus during most of his public ministry. Nowhere is it reported that Mary went to live in the desert and was persecuted there.

The other highly favored interpretation is that the "woman clothed with the sun" represents the people of God: Israel. If the woman here is Mary, who brought forth the Messiah, then Mary could be thought of as the representative of Israel.

The concept of *sign* is of enormous importance, not only here but also in the Gospel of John. Four of the seven times this word occurs in Revelation are found in these two chapters (12:1, 3; 13:13, 14; 15:1; 16:14, 19-20). In 12:1 and 3, the two signs are the woman and the dragon. In 13:13 and 14, the lamb-dragon works signs that convince the majority that the dragon is worthy of worship. In the Gospel of John, Jesus is the great sign of God who works signs intended to reveal the salvation present in Jesus. Therefore, in Jesus, *sign* and *person* are joined in a unity.

In these chapters, much the same thing is taking place. The woman and her son are God's great sign of salvation. The dragon (Satan) and the two beasts of sea and earth are countersigns or imitations of the real sign. The religious thought of Revelation 12–13 depends on this viewpoint. God reveals the good news of salvation. Subsequently, Satan and the powers of evil at his command parody and mock this sign by presenting convincing imitations.

In John's Gospel, Jesus is presented as a prophet who works signs (John 4:19; 6:14; 7:40; 9:17). This same way of thinking is present in Revelation. Prophets—even false prophets—deal in signs. In Revelation we have both Christ and an antichrist dealing in signs. Christ and the dragon are themselves signs as well. The difficulty is that both cannot be the reliable sign of the truth, and mortals have to decide which sign truly reveals God's salvation. The need for such a choice makes the situation of humans in Revelation tense and hazardous.

Revelation 12:3. The word *dragon* in the New International Version is a literal translation of the Greek word *drakon*. The word will likely give modern readers a difficult time, since dragons are a standard feature of fantasy stories. In the biblical record (Job 7:12; Psalm 74:14; Isaiah 27:1; 51:9), dragons dwell in the chaos below the sea and there threaten the tranquility of creation.

In dealing with the threat of the dragons in Revelation 12–13, the challenge is to find a means of releasing the dragon from its possibilities as a mythical creature. At the core, the dragon's threat is that of aborting the saving sign of Christ. This threat is serious and not to be reduced to a trivial game of dragons and damsels in distress.

Revelation 12:4. The conflict implicit in this verse may be the skeleton of a battle-in-heaven story, which precedes the detailed story in 12:7-9. Another, similar story is found in 9:1-6. There, a star (angel) falls from heaven and is given the key to the deep tormenting locusts, which were to prey on humans.

This story continues in chapter 20 of Revelation, where another angel seizes the dragon and locks him in the Abyss for a thousand years. Specifically, the dragon is identified there as "that ancient serpent, who is the devil, or Satan" (20:2). This action is reversed after a thousand years, and Satan is released to "deceive the nations" (20:8).

This story seems to suggest a fairly obvious, general picture of Satan's cosmic history. Satan was, from earliest time, an angel of deceit who was permitted to come and go, working evil in both heaven and earth. A crisis occurred in which Satan was exiled from heaven, taking a large company of angels with him (9:1; 12:9). From that time forward, Satan and his angels were restricted to earth. Satan's work came to a climax in the attempt to subvert the salvation brought by Christ (12:4b-5).

The war with Michael, described in detail in 12:7-9, would then be the attempt of Satan to follow Christ to heaven and continue his efforts to reverse the redemption of the Incarnation. This attempt fails when Satan and his angels are defeated by the champion angel, Michael, and his angelic army. Satan then realizes that the church is the continuing presence of Christ on earth and turns his full wrath on its faithful.

Revelation 12:5. The image of Christ ruling with "an iron scepter" may be an allusion to the dream and its interpretation in Daniel 2:31-45. King Nebuchadnezzar dreamed of an image made of five substances, a head of gold, chest and arms of silver, belly and thighs of bronze, legs of iron, and feet made with a mixture of iron and clay. According to Daniel's interpretation, Nebuchadnezzar was the head. The feet of clay and iron represented a future, divided kingdom (Daniel 2:41) that would be destroyed by a kingdom designed by God. This kingdom is represented by a rock "cut out, but not by human hands" (Daniel 2:34, 45) that would crush and destroy the four kingdoms to follow that of Nebuchadnezzar and the Babylonian Empire.

With this background, we can see how this simple claim (one "who will rule all the nations with an iron scepter") relies on concepts taken from Daniel. Put in this context, the full idea might be paraphrased, "In the birth of Christ, the kingdoms of this world have been smashed by the power of the Incarnation."

The Old Testament literary quality of this phrase comes through in the words the writer uses that come from Psalm 2:9: "You will break them with a rod of iron; / you will dash them to pieces like pottery."

Revelation 12:9. Revelation 12 uses a fascinating array of names for Satan. *Satan* is the word most common to Hebrew readers. The *devil* is from the Greek term *diabolos*. The root meaning of *diabolos* is "slanderer." This root meaning is defined more completely in the next verse as "the accuser of our brothers and sisters" (12:10). Other names include "that ancient serpent" and "the great dragon."

In Revelation 12–13, the aspect of Satan's personality examined most closely is contained in the name "the deceiver" (see 13:14), rendered in 12:9 as the one "who leads the whole world astray" (12:9). The picture of evil in Revelation 12–13 is close to that in the apocalyptic passages of Matthew 24 and Mark 13. In the Gospels, Jesus says to his disciples, "Watch out that no one deceives you. Many will come in my name, claiming, 'I am he,' and will deceive many" (Mark 13:5-6; see also Matthew 24:4-5). This idea is really a good summary of most of Revelation 13, and the key idea of subtlety is the same in both places. The agent who leads the faithful astray is someone who looks and sounds like an authentic prophet or even an authentic Christ. Those who claim to be another Christ usually assert that Christ has come again but remains hidden; or they talk of an alternative incarnation for the people who missed it the first time; or they claim in subtle suggestions that they are divine. These claims, say both Jesus and John, are to be flatly disbelieved and vigorously rejected.

Revelation 12:10-12. The place of Satan's war against the saints has changed, but this is not particularly good news. A part of Satan's cosmic strategy has been defeated. The attempt to destroy the One who brings universal salvation, Jesus Christ, has failed. Satan is cast from heaven and no longer can advocate against the faith by means of his insidious whisper campaign in the company of heaven. Soon, we will also learn that, even when limited to earth, Satan will fail to destroy the church. All this is good news. The bad news is that Satan has become more vicious and intense in the deception worked against earth's faithful. The intensity is motivated by the fact that Satan's time is just about up—and he knows it (12:12).

Revelation 12:13-17. While the story of the dragon's pursuit of the woman is provocative, it also alludes to other events. We can hear echoes of the wilderness wandering theme of the Old Testament, as well as see connections with the flight of the Holy Family to Egypt, and Jesus' forty days and nights in the wilderness while tempted by Satan. Probably all these associations are intended by John.

Given the vicious persecution of Christians in the Roman Empire, beginning with Nero, the message is quite clear. Just as Satan tried to divert Israel and Mary, Joseph, and Jesus in their desert sojourns, so also Satan will continue to seek and destroy the offspring of this holy history, the faithful followers of the kingdom of God. The wilderness holds many associations for Christians. The meaning closest to the surface here is probably that of the forty years of wandering in the wilderness after Israel's disobedience. This association has a twofold theme: the people of God are sustained miraculously by God (e.g., by manna), yet the wilderness represents the constant threat of separation from God. These two necessary elements of the wilderness theme struggle with each other with great creativity.

The word *offspring* in verse 17, as a description of spiritual descendants, is found elsewhere in the New Testament (Romans 4:13; Galatians 3:29; Hebrews 2:16). Here the term refers to those who are Christ's spiritual descendants, after the fashion described in Romans 8:15-17 ("We are God's children.").

In the rescue of the woman, the earth appears almost as a living, conscious being: "The earth helped the woman by opening its mouth," (12:16). This description, together with the theme of a river of water acting as the enemy, recalls the atmosphere of Creation in Genesis 2:4-9 where humans are closely connected with the earth, almost to the extent of being partners. The threat of destruction by water recalls the Flood.

Revelation 13:1-4. The beast of the sea is conjured up by Satan as his major means of making war on the earth. This fact is not immediately obvious but becomes so at the time the beast from the earth appears (13:11-12). The connection of thoughts here is interesting. Satan's war is waged by supplying a figure who leads humans astray, convincing them to worship the beast. War is waged by means of worship. Beneath this war is an idea we see often in Revelation. The most essential human response possible is the praise of God. This response is predicted by the nature of creation. Since all things are made by God, the essence of creation is best reflected in praise of the Creator. If this praise can be changed by evil into idolatry (i.e., the creation worshiping itself rather than worshiping the One who created it), then creation has been corrupted. Satan shrewdly realizes that idolatry is the best means of deceiving the human family.

The enormous authority of the beast from the sea is based on the impulse to worship it as God; not giving in to the praise of the beast is the heart and soul of conquering Satan.

Revelation 13:8. While these words may suggest a rigid kind of predestination, John does not intend that meaning. Such a doctrine did not exist at the time of the writing of Revelation. The verse does suggest that the redeemed are known by God even prior to Creation.

Revelation 13:9. This verse gives a stark warning. When Jesus sought to convey the mystery of the kingdom to his disciples, he concluded his teaching with similar words (Mark 4:9): "Whoever has ears, let them hear."

Revelation 13:10. The poetry of this statement may appear to be a direct quotation from another part of Scripture, but it is not. However, Jeremiah 15:2 is similar: "Those destined for death, to death; / those for the sword, to the sword; / those for starvation, to starvation; / those for captivity, to captivity." The poetry is haunting but can be reduced to a single idea: Sad though it may be, the time is approaching when many will suffer and die.

Rarely does John directly address those who are hearing Revelation read to them. Therefore the "call" for endurance and faithfulness must be viewed as a shocking interruption of the narrative flow. The crisis the prophet senses approaching seems to move him to step out of character as narrator and say directly to his audience, "Watch yourselves!"

Revelation 13:11-17. The emphasis on the wounded-but-healed head of the beast (13:3, 12, 14) confirms this figure as the antichrist. Put more accurately, the beast is a counterfeit Christ. The head, wounded but healed, is a parody of Christ crucified and risen. This being the case, the second beast (13:11) is the false prophet who acts as priest of what can only be called the sea beast religion. We get more detail here on how false prophets work: trickery and gimmicks figure high in convincing humans that the beast from the sea ought to be worshiped.

John gives us yet another keen insight based on simple economics. Whoever controls the means of trade controls all else. A false religion could become quite popular if it were the only means of obtaining food, shelter, and clothing.

Revelation 13:18. Even before the New Testament existed as a recognized collection of authoritative scripture, discussions took place about the identity of the antichrist. The number 666 has fascinated readers virtually from the day Revelation was written. When human enemies are made to fit the number 666, this only serves to entrench us in the sin of inherited prejudices. Irenaeus, the first great theologian of the church, wrote at length about this problem as early as the second century. His advice is, if anything, more valuable today:

It is . . . more certain, and less hazardous, to await the fulfillment of the prophecy, than to be making surmises, and casting about for any names that may present themselves, inasmuch as many names can be found possessing the number mentioned; and the same question will, after all, remain unsolved.[1]

DIMENSION THREE: WHAT DOES THE BIBLE MEAN TO ME?

Revelation 12–13

One characteristic of apocalyptic thought is a direct contrast of good and evil, with no shades of difference. Our experience tells us, however, that good laws, good institutions, good people, and good ideas can often be used for an evil purpose. A number of the questions posed in the participant book may bring simplistic, right vs. wrong answers. The danger of answering in this way is, of course, that we may decide that good is evil. Or, we may allow serious forces of evil to prosper by calling them good.

History has taught us to be cautious about quick and easy decisions about people and events. Often we "repent at leisure" those decisions made without careful thought. An example of this kind of decision is the practice of slavery. At one time, the enslavement of persons was seen as a foundation stone of civilized nations. Without slaves, some thought, economic growth would be impossible. The system of slavery was supported by religious convictions crafted out of the Bible. In other words, with hardly a murmur of protest, an economic system based on a great evil was enshrined as good in the eyes of Christians. Now we realize how terribly wrong and evil such a system was.

Revelation invites the reader to look beneath the disguise of evil. And, because the character of evil is subtle deceitfulness, we will usually find that the hidden evil lies within ourselves, those opinions we hold most dearly, and the systems we have come to think of as good.

---

1 Irenaeus, "Against Heresies," in *The Ante-Nicene Fathers*, vol. 1 (Charles Scribner's Sons, 1905, American reprint of the Edinburgh edition), 559.

They were purchased from among mankind and offered as firstfruits to God and the Lamb. (14:4c)

8

SINGING A NEW SONG
Revelation 14

DIMENSION ONE:
WHAT DOES THE BIBLE SAY?

Answer these questions by reading Revelation 14

1. What do the 144,000 have inscribed on their foreheads? (14:1)
   The Lamb's name and God's name are written there.

2. How did the voice from heaven sound? (14:2)
   The voice sounded like rushing waters, loud thunder, and many harps being played.

3. Who is allowed to learn the new song? (14:3)
   Only the 144, 000 are permitted to learn the new song.

4. List the six different ways the 144,000 are described. (14:4-5)
   The 144,000 are described in six ways; they: (1) are chaste, (2) follow the Lamb, (3) have been "purchased from among mankind," (4) have been offered to God as firstfruits, (5) are without deceit, and (6) are blameless.

5. What does the first angel say to all the earth's people? (14:7)
   He tells them to fear God, give God glory, and worship God.

6. What is the second angel's message? (14:8)
   This angel announces the fall of Babylon.

7. What does the third angel announce? (14:9-11)

   The third angel announces the coming judgment of God's wrath on all those who have received the mark of the beast.

8. Who is pronounced blessed by the Spirit? (14:13)

   Those who die in the Lord are blessed "from now on."

9. Who appears on a white cloud, and how is he described? (14:14)

   The "one like a son of man" comes wearing a golden crown and holding a sickle in his hand.

10. What does the "one like a son of man" do with his sickle? (14:15-16)

    Following the exhortation of yet another angel, he swings his sickle over the earth and reaps the harvest, now fully ripe.

11. Who else has a sharp sickle? (14:17)

    An angel comes out of the temple in heaven with a sharp sickle.

12. Who is the last angel described in this scene? (14:18)

    This angel comes out from the altar and is known as the one "who had charge of the fire."

13. What does this angel do? (14:18)

    The angel in charge of the fire tells the angel from the temple of heaven to harvest the "clusters of grapes from the earth's vine."

14. Where is the winepress of God located? (14:20)

    The winepress is "outside the city."

15. What does the winepress produce? (14:20)

    The winepress produces a flow of blood of immense proportions.

DIMENSION TWO:
WHAT DOES THE BIBLE MEAN?

Revelation 14:1. The Lamb standing on Mount Zion with the band of the redeemed is a preview of the final scene of the new Jerusalem coming down from God (21:2). References to Mount Zion are rare in the New Testament, and the use here reminds us of the constant echoes between the Old Testament prophets and Revelation. The reference to Mount Zion, a place enshrined in the hearts and minds of those who know the Hebrew Scriptures well, says in effect, "God is not only in the heavenly temple; God is present also on earth."

Revelation 14:2-3. While John does not say so, this scene is like those we have witnessed earlier that take place in the presence of God's throne (review the descriptions in 4:1-6; 5:6-14). In Revelation, the center of activity is the heavenly throne. The action in heaven that John sees has an impact on earth. John's vision is a visual way of saying that God is in command of the universe. The script of John's vision pivots on these throne scenes: rushing to, orbiting around, hovering in the midst of, and streaming out of the throne of God.

When the Lamb stands near this throne, the visual tapestry is complete. This tapestry portrays an all-powerful and transcendent God who is directing the destiny of our whole cosmos toward purposes held hidden from before the beginning. The Son of God, appearing frequently as the Lamb, carries out the mission of God, not in subjection to or conflict with the Creator, but in perfect obedience to this eternal design.

Revelation 14:4-5. The Lamb is also a shepherd (7:17). Therefore, it is not odd that the redeemed follow the Lamb. The word *follow* is found often in the Gospels and is used as a virtual synonym for "be a disciple." Here, the 144,000 have left earthly disruptions to follow the Lamb in another existence. This image ought not to be pressed too hard, but it does tantalize the imagination. Does discipleship continue after death? If the essence of discipleship is learning about salvation won in Christ, could it not be said that living with Christ involves learning even after death? This concept offers a fresh dimension; for other parts of the New Testament suggest that on being received by Christ, all knowledge is revealed.

The key idea of redemption depends on an exchange in which one thing is given for another. For example, in the ancient world, an indentured servant was redeemed—rescued from slavery—by payment of a cash bond. While no formal doctrines of redemption are stated in the New Testament, the outcome of the crucifixion is sometimes described as a redeeming act (1 Corinthians 6:20a; 2 Peter 2:1).

Redemption is a favorite idea of Revelation but is not fully developed. In later theology, elaborate theories of atonement were constructed. At the core of these was frequently the idea that God redeemed humans from Satan at the price of Jesus' death. This idea is not even implied in Revelation and should not be assumed by readers who know about such theories of atonement. Rather, the redeemed are called "firstfruits," that is, the first of those redeemed who remained faithful, even when tested by death. They are a premium pledge of all those who will follow. To this extent, the redeemed are held out as examples of faith.

Celibacy is probably not to be taken as a general condition for being considered faithful. In light of early Christian evidence, celibacy was not required of followers. Rather, behind the praise for undefiled men lies the fact that many cults of the Roman Empire required consort with female prostitutes. Christians are to abstain from such immoral sexual practices, even when supposedly justified on the basis of religious beliefs. One of the values of Revelation's place in Christian thought is to point out the impossibility of such practices being followed on a religious basis.

Revelation 14:6-7. Here again we see the universalism of John's vision. The angel's message is for all who dwell on earth. No one—good or evil—is excluded from the judgment. "Fear God" means to hold God in awe. The praise called for here is the expected response to the arrival of the hour for the Last Judgment. God is also to be worshiped as the Creator, the One "who made the heavens, the earth, the sea and the springs of water" (14:7).

Revelation 14:8. Much attention will be given to Babylon in John's vision of chapters 17–18. John is greatly indebted to the extensive oracles against Babylon found in Jeremiah 51 and to frequent mentions in Ezekiel, Daniel, and other Old Testament prophets.

Babylon is a commanding symbol of devastation because of Israel's tragic history with that powerful enemy. In the days of Jeremiah, Babylon destroyed Judah, the temple, and the monarchy, and took captive royalty and leaders from all levels of society and religion. Ezekiel was taken captive with this group, and much of his prophecy concerns the consequence of that captivity.

A great range of literature within the Hebrew Scriptures comes out of the period of Babylonian exile, and Jewish thinking was changed for all time by this experience. Daniel, written well after the captivity, uses Babylon and the story of interaction with its king, Nebuchadnezzar, as a means of dealing with a more contemporary threat, Antiochus IV, who held Israel ransom through cruel occupation.

Revelation follows in Daniel's footsteps with great artistry. For John, Babylon could be only the dreaded Roman Empire. But John's thought is even more subtle; a bit of Babylon threatens in every corner of life.

Verse 8 poses a particular problem. Because the language here is so close to that of 17:2 and 18:3, the exact symbolic nature of the wine in Babylon's cup is unclear. From 17:2, the wine would seem to be of "her" making, namely idolatry (conveyed by the metaphor of fornication or harlotry). Still, in 14:9-11, we see another wine in a cup, the wine of God's wrath. If that wine is the same, and, therefore, the same cup of anger from God, then we would have a true irony. Babylon intoxicates the nations with the dreadful wine of God's wrath. In other words, Babylon is the unwitting servant of God. When persons drink from the cup, they are doomed.

Revelation 14:10b. Why are the worshipers of a false God tormented in the presence of Christ and the angels? The answer lies in the need for witnesses to justice. A peculiar aspect of both the Old Testament prophets and Revelation is to call witnesses to see that God's justice has been done. This often takes the appearance of a formal trial in which various parts of creation "stand in" as witnesses or jury. Here, the Lamb and angels serve that purpose. This desire for witness in God's court is motivated, not by the need to have God's righteousness attested to, but simply to emphasize the truth of God's judgment.

Revelation 14:11. The "smoke of their torment" is a deliberate contrast with the "smoke of the incense" symbolizing the prayers of the faithful (8:4; 5:8).

The judgment conveyed to the beast worshipers is a preliminary glimpse. In Revelation 19:20-21, the battle between Christ and this group is described in detail.

Revelation 14:12. This verse is an excellent summary of Revelation's message. John's vision is well designed to convince the suffering saints of the Roman Empire that God is in control of the destiny of the world and its history. To serve God by keeping the law given to Moses and perfected by Jesus of Nazareth is not only worthwhile, but also essential to life itself.

The meaning of the word translated *endurance* can also be conveyed by words such as *patience, fortitude, steadfastness,* and *perseverance.* In the Gospels, Jesus is the example of perfect perseverance. This perseverance is shown especially in his approach to the cross: he endures betrayal, unjust manipulation of Jewish and Roman law, beatings, and death. No wonder this Christian response to injustice and oppression receives such a place of honor.

Revelation 14:13. This blessing (or beatitude) is an echo of 6:9-11. John shows a touching and consistent concern in Revelation for those who die under persecution. The blessing may include all Christians who die in faithfulness, whether or not as the result of martyrdom. This issue is decided on the basis of what it means to die "in the Lord." If the sense is of following the example of Jesus, then this beatitude limits its blessing to martyrs.

Does John in Revelation believe that a Christian's works play a role in salvation? Several passages mention deeds at work. In Revelation 2:2, the church of Ephesus is told, "I know your deeds, your hard work and your perseverance." Here, it is quite clear that works are Christian virtues (such as endurance, described above). This suggests that, in Revelation's view, deeds or works are evidence of Christ's presence working in the saints; they are not the source of salvation. Finally, these works do not go before the faithful to obtain a place in heaven but accompany them.

Revelation 14:14-16. The title "son of man" as a designation of Jesus Christ is common to the New Testament; it has not become a favorite name for Christ, and it is seldom used outside scholarly circles today. Still, Jesus spoke of himself using this title on many occasions (e.g., Matthew 8:20; 9:6; 10:23; 11:19; 12:8; 13:37; 16:13; 17:9; 19:28; 20:18; 24:27; 25:31; 26:64). The fact that the Gospels and Revelation agree on the importance of this title reminds us that Revelation is not from the fringes of early Christianity but close to the heart of it. Only recently have scholars come to appreciate this fact, which has caused a fresh and helpful reappraisal of this book. This title for Jesus is used in many ways, but perhaps the most significant is reflected in this historic saying of Jesus as reported by Matthew: "The Son of Man is going to come in his Father's glory with his angels, and then he will reward each person according to what they have done" (Matthew 16:27).

Read side-by-side with this saying, the echoes in Revelation 14:14-16 are astounding. They are even more astounding because we do not know that John ever read Matthew's Gospel.

One of the crucial elements in Jesus' faith was that of the coming of the Son of Man in judgment. The unity between Revelation and the faith of Jesus on this point is a witness to this book's place in preserving ancient traditions that lie at the base of Christianity.

Revelation 14:17-20. The Old Testament prophets, John the Baptist, and Jesus often used the extended metaphors of vineyard and harvest as ways of speaking about God's judgment. John 15 is a classic example of an extended metaphor in which Christ is the vine and the disciples his branches.

Jesus is the wine of the Lord's Supper, as well as the bread. The connection between the wine and blood is easily made; since the blood of Christ, shed on the cross, is symbolic of his essence. Many of the specific wordings of this passage are close to, if not modeled on, pronouncements of various Old Testament prophets (e.g., Joel 3:13).

The fascinating detail that this judgment scene takes place "outside the city" (14:20) raises an issue relevant to the entire chapter: We cannot reconcile groups, places, and times between this chapter and the rest of Revelation. The entire chapter is filled with references backward and forward in the book. Revelation 14 provides an excellent setting for reaffirming that the most fruitful uses of this book do not include forcing each part into a doctrinal scheme that must work together for all its parts.

DIMENSION THREE: WHAT DOES THE BIBLE MEAN TO ME?

Revelation 14

(NOTE: Participant book has questions related to 14:1-5, 6-7, 8-11, 12-13, 14-20.) From this point forward, Revelation will deal in greater and greater detail with the belief in divine judgment that leads to suffering for millions. At the same time, John puts consistent emphasis on the salvation of the saints who endure in the midst of persecution. Revelation depends on a stark contrast between a small, persecuted minority and a sea of opposition, idolatry, and immorality. Revelation is, to a certain extent, a social statement concerning "we who are righteous" and "they who are evil."

At another level, this statement is too simple an analysis of Revelation's perspective. John is quite clear that all worship—"ours" and "theirs"—has the potential for idolatry. John may have in mind that Christian worship is constantly in danger of becoming idolatry. In other words, the enemy may be *us*, not *them*.

In discussing this chapter and the questions raised in the participant book, you may wish to ask questions such as these: How do we know whether the mark on our forehead is the name of God or of the beast? How do we know whether the song of our heart is an old, sad song or the new song of the redeemed? How do we know whether the cup we drink is the life-giving sacrificial blood of the Lamb or the cup of God's anger?

"Go, pour out the seven bowls of God's wrath on the earth." (16:1)

9

SEVEN BOWLS OF WRATH

Revelation 15–16

DIMENSION ONE:
WHAT DOES THE BIBLE SAY?

Answer these questions by reading Revelation 15

1. What was the sign John the prophet saw in heaven? (15:1)
   He saw "seven angels with the seven last plagues."

2. Who stands beside the sea of glass? (15:2a)
   All those who have triumphed over the beast stand beside the sea of glass.

3. What are they doing? (15:2b-3)
   They are playing harps and singing "the song of God's servant Moses and of the Lamb."

4. What does the song foresee? (15:4c)
   All the nations of the world will come to worship God.

5. Where do the angels with the plagues come from? (15:5-6)
   They come from "the tabernacle of the covenant law" in heaven.

6. Who gives the angels the golden bowls full of wrath? (15:7)
   One of the four living creatures gives them the bowls.

7. What happens in the temple after this? (15:8)

The temple is filled with smoke, and no one can enter.

Answer these questions by reading Revelation 16

8. What is the first plague poured out of the golden bowl by the angel? (16:2)

"Ugly, festering sores" afflict the beast worshipers.

9. What is the second plague poured out? (16:3)

The sea turns to a blood-like substance, and every living thing in the sea dies.

10. How is the third plague like the second? (16:4)

The third plague is the same as the second but affects fresh water.

11. How are the two plagues of blood infecting water explained? (16:5-7)

Because the saints and prophets have been murdered by those who follow the beast, God has given the beast worshipers "blood to drink."

12. What is the fourth plague? (16:8)

The power of the sun is increased to allow humans to be tormented by scorching heat.

13. Who do the followers of the beast blame for the plagues? (16:9)

They blame God, not themselves, and therefore do not repent.

14. Against what is the fifth plague directed? (16:10)

The fifth plague is poured on the throne of the beast.

15. What is the result of this plague? (16:10-11)

The plague darkens the kingdom of the beast, and this sends panic among his followers.

16. On what does the sixth plague fall? (16:12)

The sixth plague falls on the river Euphrates, drying it up completely.

17. Why is the river dried up? (16:12)

The dry riverbed is made ready for the great battle, making it easy for the armies of the East to cross the Euphrates.

18. How do the dragon, the beast, and the false prophet respond to this plague? (16:13-14)

They send out three evil spirits whose task is to deceive the world's nations into doing battle with God.

19. Where is the final battle to be held? (16:16)

The battle is to be at Armageddon.

20. What takes place when the seventh golden bowl is poured out? (16:18-21)

A series of natural disasters, more devastating than ever before experienced in history, takes place. These disasters include massive earthquakes that dislodge islands, level mountains, and destroy cities. Also, enormous hailstones fall on people.

21. Who is particularly singled out for destruction? (16:19)

"Babylon the Great" experiences the full force of God's wrath.

DIMENSION TWO: WHAT DOES THE BIBLE MEAN?

Revelation 15:1. The first sign was the vision of the woman clothed with the sun (chap. 12). Now a special place of importance is given to the seven plagues, as they are the signs of the conclusion of judgment. The two chapters narrating the seven plagues (15–16) will be followed by two chapters (17–18) of oracles against the harlot of Babylon. Then John begins the narration of Christ's final victory over Satan (19–20). These opening words convey a sense of finality.

Revelation 15:2-4. John often will report an aspect of his vision in comparative language and then move on to call that vision by the name of the comparison ("what looked like a sea of glass

. . . standing beside the sea," 15:2). This literary technique must be followed carefully in the text if you want to avoid confusion.

In describing the seal of his vision, John says it "looked like a sea of glass glowing with fire." We have already seen the sea of heaven with John in 4:6, but here the flickering color of fire is added. Perhaps John is trying to describe a body of water that is so smooth and clear that it reflects like glass. The dancing of flame may refer to movement or reflections of lightning flashing on the surface of the lake.

The song of Moses, recorded in Exodus 15:1-18, resembles this hymn of praise only in majesty and atmosphere. John does not use a direct quotation. Some scholars suggest that John heard this choir first sing the old song of Moses and then this new song composed by the Lamb. In any event, the remarkable part of this scene is that Moses is viewed as one of God's faithful servants, along with the martyred faithful of earth, and that Moses and Christ are characterized as heavenly choral masters.

The suggestion that the ascended Jesus is a maker of music is a rich and expansive metaphor with many possibilities. At the very least, this picture suggests that some aspects of service to God and understanding of creation can be fulfilled only by the writing, playing, and singing of music. We have met this attitude previously, but here the point is made stronger.

The fourth line of the hymn presents a textual problem that scholars have debated for centuries. God is either "King of the ages" or "King of the nations." Textual evidence is equivocal, but the unmistakable wording of verse 4, "All nations will come / and worship before you," gives support to reading *nations* in 15:3, thus creating a parallelism.

Revelation 15:5. When John says, "I looked," we know that something of great significance is about to happen.

We have been used to dealing with the heavenly temple, but the building mentioned in verse 5 is a great mystery. Of course, a mobile tent of worship was used by Israel in the desert wanderings. But this tabernacle or portable sanctuary was quite different from the temples of Solomon and Herod. Hebrews 8–9 includes a sustained study on the tent-sanctuary of Israel's nomadic period. But this verse gives the only mention of the tabernacle in Revelation.

Revelation 15:7. Exactly what these bowls look like is unclear, but a difference between bowl and cup is carefully maintained by John for some reason. Some have suggested that the bowls are most appropriately thought of as basins, shallow and wide at the mouth. This shape would result in more instantaneous emptying out.

Revelation 16:2. Twice in these chapters, the beast's image is singled out for special treatment (15:2; 16:2). John clearly is outraged at the image of the beast, because it is a symbol of idolatry. To conquer the beast is to conquer its image. This idea might include resistance to the power and drama of the image in ritual, beauty, symbolism, and perhaps even in music.

Revelation 16:5-7. This hymn contains several interesting and subtle details. God is just in all judgments. If God were only just and not also all-powerful, we could have no confidence in the hope for a just outcome. John has clearly established by now, however, that God is powerful beyond all powers that exist, because God created all else. This affirmation is hinted at in the second line of the hymn. "Who are and who were" (v. 5) is a poetic way of saying that "God is eternal." Then comes the ironic twist: Human beings have poured out the blood of the prophets and saints; therefore, God has poured out the bowls of wrath.

The final lines are something like a response, such as might be found in a litany. The angel's song of praise ends with verse 6, but the response—"Yes, Lord God Almighty, / true and just are your judgments"—comes from the altar in verse 7. Who are these voices? They are, we learned in 6:9-11, the martyrs of the faith who dwell under the altar of sacrifice in the heavenly temple. We heard them, with John, crying out for their blood to be avenged. Here, as a liturgical choir, we hear them again, avenged, praising God for the justice of divine judgment. In this way John deftly picks up a theme planted earlier and completes part of a literary cycle. More important, he brings forward the plot in a kind of momentary climax.

Earlier, Moses was called "God's servant" (15:3), and here, the prophets of the Old Testament are identified as martyrs (16:6). This adulation of the prophetic tradition recalls the mini-history of the prophets told in 11:4-13. Verse 11:6b establishes a direct connection between this section of chapter 16 and the power of prophecy: "They have power to turn the waters into blood and to strike the earth with every kind of plague as often as they want."

The connection reveals another level of ironic artistry on John's part. Note how many of these plagues are modeled after the plagues visited on Egypt through Moses (Exodus 7–11). The message of God in these plagues is that, while humans were able to silence and kill the prophets, the time is fast approaching when judgment will come by means of prophetic acts. In this way Moses and Elijah are made present realities in the world's circumstances. This reality is, indeed, bitter irony for those who scoffed at the prophets throughout the centuries.

Revelation 16:9. John attempts to point out that repentance does not always follow divine punishment, as might be expected. This truth also links with the history of prophetic ministry. The people and their leaders refuse to learn from their experiences of God's justice. This theme is consistent throughout Scripture. Revelation continues in this conviction and builds the story of final judgment around it.

Revelation 16:10-11. The results of the fifth plague are mingled with those of the first for some reason. While potentially confusing in syntax, the meaning is clear. People chewed their tongues in pain (not anguish) because of the repugnant sores of the first plague. The results of the darkness visited on the beast's kingdom are not specified.

Revelation 16:13. The dragon, the beast, and the false prophet are described collectively as three evil spirits. The third beast is identified for the first time as "the false prophet" of the second beast and its image. The mention of frogs recalls still another plague on the Egyptians (Exodus 8:1-6). This likeness does not completely explain the interesting change of images from evil spirits to frogs. However, in some Eastern religions, well known to the Roman Empire, evil gods took the form of frogs. This fact may explain the strange jump from one image to another.

Revelation 16:14. The final battle will be a "great day" for "God Almighty" simply because on that day the fullness of divine justice and power will be seen.

Revelation 16:15. This interlude is an intrusion into the narration of the vision and is given as a direct exhortation to those who hear the book read. Christ speaks directly to the hearer in the first person. The image of Christ returning as a thief is yet another firm connection with Jesus in the Gospels. In Matthew 24:42-44, Jesus compares his return with a thief coming in the night (see also 1 Thessalonians 5:2-4).

The interlude includes yet another beatitude (see 14:13) in which watchfulness is blessed. The exhortation to remain awake is a constant theme in the Gospels and always in connection with the return of Christ (Matthew 24:42; 25:13; 26:40; Mark 13:35, 37). This beatitude is the second firm connection in this verse with the Gospel tradition of Jesus speaking about his return.

No place in the Gospels connects conveniently with the metaphor of *nakedness* as unprepared to meet Jesus when he returns, as is clearly the meaning here. However, we do know the fascinating story, told only by Mark (14:51-52), in which an anonymous young man fled the scene of Jesus' arrest and, leaving behind his garment, went into the night naked.

Revelation 16:16. The name Armageddon is given here as if it is a well-known place in Palestine. Actually, the name appears nowhere else within Scripture or outside it.

John's narration of the final battle between Christ and Satan is modeled on the Gog-Magog battle in Ezekiel 38–39. John tells the story sketchily in Revelation 20:7-11. In Ezekiel, this battle was to have taken place in the vicinity of the "mountains of Israel" (Ezekiel 39:2, 4).

Revelation 16:17. With an almost audible sigh of relief, the end of Rome is finally declared with, "It is done!" This proclamation creates a turning point in Revelation's development. The proclamation reaches back to 10:5-6, in which the mighty angel declares that "there will be no more delay." But we have already seen dramatic delay, and more delay of the same kind awaits us. The delay, however, is for dramatic effect and is not meant to convey vacillation on God's part.

Revelation 16:19. When John describes what takes place, he uses an intense phrase—"the fury of his wrath." This phrase contains two words, both of which can be translated "wrath." This sentence, then, describes a doubling up of wrath. The idea of making pronouncements more frightening by piling up terms is a technique the Old Testament prophets often used. For example, see Jeremiah 4:26 and Hosea 11:9. John uses this device again in Revelation 19:15c: "the fury of the wrath of God Almighty."

DIMENSION THREE: WHAT DOES THE BIBLE MEAN TO ME?

Revelation 15–16

(NOTE: Participant Book has questions related to 15:3-4, 5-8; 16:1-11, 12-14, 15.) Several themes in Revelation 15–16 invite discussion: the universal dimension of God's rule, the command of God over cosmic principles of justice, the punishment inherent in idolatry, the place of worship in the language of faith, and vigilance in the faith while waiting for the fullness of Christ's kingdom.

Several passages in these two chapters affirm that the eventual outcome of God's judgment will be the ingathering of all people into the orbit of God's worship. The theology in Revelation has no place for a tribal religion that keeps to itself. The goal is that all nations on earth should confess the rightness of God's sovereign rule and praise God in joyful acclamation. John presents absolute intolerance for the many cults and religions of Hellenistic civilization.

What are we to make of this attitude in light of our present circumstance? More and more we are aware of the global importance of religion in conflicts of political and economic life in our world. Much of the tension that exists today is based in religious conflict and differences. Do not attitudes such as those seen in these chapters simply add to the problems? The answer, of course, lies in the goal of God's justice. God's justice does not seek the advancement of any particular nation at the expense of another but the establishment of a reign of righteousness for all persons.

Rome's destruction was seen by John as a necessary outcome of a reign of immorality, oppression, and idolatry. In other words, the failure of Rome's religious vision brought Rome's downfall. This conclusion is no different from that of the Old Testament prophets who were as quick to condemn Israel as they were to pronounce God's judgment on unrighteous pagan nations who surrounded Israel.

When John wrote Revelation, there was no Christian nation in existence to which he could speak. Christians lived in scattered bands across the Roman Empire and were still a small minority. Likely John would have found much to condemn in later Christian Rome, as indeed he could in our and other so-called Christian nations. Don't shy away from difficult conversations or controversial ideas that may come from discussion of the questions in the participant's book or of the way in which religion plays a role in the political and economic conflicts in our world today. What would John say to us today? Are we called to speak a voice of prophecy to our world? What are we called to say?

"I will explain to you the mystery of the woman." (17:7b)

10

BABYLON IS FALLEN

Revelation 17–18

DIMENSION ONE:
WHAT DOES THE BIBLE SAY?

Answer these questions by reading Revelation 17

1. Who is the woman who sits on many waters? (17:1)
    She is described as a "great prostitute."

2. What is the charge against her? (17:2)
    She has committed adultery with kings of the earth and other earth inhabitants.

3. Where is the woman seated next? (17:3)
    She is seen seated on a scarlet beast with seven heads and ten horns.

4. What does she hold in her hand? (17:4)
    She holds a cup filled with "abominable things and the filth of her adulteries."

5. What is her name, and how do we know it? (17:5)
    Written on her forehead is the mysterious name, "BABYLON THE GREAT / THE MOTHER OF PROSTITUTES / AND OF THE ABOMINATIONS OF THE EARTH."

6. Who interprets the meaning of the mystery to John? (17:7)
    An angel interprets the mystery for John.

7. According to the angel, how are the following parts of the vision to be interpreted? (17:8-15):
    a. The beast with seven heads and ten horns? (17:8a)
    The beast is the same beast connected with the Abyss in 11:7.

    b. The inhabitants of the earth? (17:8b)
    They are those who do not have their names written in the book of life, or all those who worship the beast.

    c. The seven heads on the beast? (17:9-10)
    They are seven kings and "seven hills on which the woman sits."

    d. The ten horns? (17:12)
    They are ten kings who will in the future receive power for a short period.

    e. The waters on which the prostitute sits? (17:15)
    They represent a multitude of people made up of many nations and languages.

8. What does the angel say will happen to the prostitute? (17:16)
    The angel says that the beast and the ten kings will destroy her.

9. Why will this happen? (17:17)
    God will motivate the kings to give their power to the beast instead of to the prostitute to fulfill the requirements of justice.

10. Who is this woman? (17:18)
    She is "the great city that rules over the kings of the earth"—Rome.

Answer these questions by reading Revelation 18

11. What lives in Babylon, according to the angel with great authority? (18:2)
    Demons, "every impure spirit," and "every unclean bird," and "every unclean and detestable animal" dwell there.

12. Who has been contaminated by Babylon? (18:3)

    She has given drink of her adulteries to all nations, has committed adultery with the kings of the earth, and has fed the greed of merchants.

13. To whom does the next voice speak? (18:4)

    The people of God, "my people," are called away from Babylon.

14. Why is it important for the people to get out of Babylon? (18:4)

    They must leave, or they might take part in her sins and receive her judgment.

15. On what principle will Babylon be punished? (18:6)

    She will be repaid double for her sins.

16. What does Babylon think about herself? (18:7)

    She deludes herself by thinking that she is as God and will never fall.

17. Who will weep for Babylon? (18:9)

    All the kings of the earth with whom she has consorted will "weep and mourn" over Babylon.

18. Why do the merchants of the earth weep for her? (18:11-17a)

    The merchants weep for Babylon because they no longer have buyers for their costly goods.

19. Why do those who earn their living from the sea weep for the destruction of the city? (18:17b-19)

    They weep because they know that this destruction will mean a loss of the shipping trade.

20. While kings, merchants, and seafaring men weep, who is asked to rejoice? (18:20)

    The company of heaven, people of God, apostles, and prophets are called to rejoice in the judgment of God.

21. In the next action of the vision, what does the angel do? (18:21)

As an illustration, the angel drops a great millstone into the sea and says that, like the millstone, so will be Babylon.

22. What will no longer be found in Babylon? (18:22-23)

The sounds of music, the work of crafters, the sound of grinding millstones, the shining of lamps, and the sounds of wedding parties will no longer be found there.

23. What is the final reason given for Babylon's fall? (18:24)

Babylon shed the blood of the prophets and God's holy people and many others on earth.

DIMENSION TWO:
WHAT DOES THE BIBLE MEAN?

These two chapters of Revelation are two of the most confusing in the entire book. They both deal with only one subject: the sins of Rome and prophecies of doom that look forward to Rome's fall. The prophet John of Patmos thought a great deal like the Old Testament prophets, especially Ezekiel, Joel, Isaiah, and Jeremiah. He also had read the Book of Daniel many times. In fact, he was so familiar with these books that he often fell back on their ideas, images, symbols, and metaphors when expressing what he experienced in his vision. Nothing makes this knowledge of Old Testament prophets more evident than his choice of Babylon as a secret symbol for imperial Rome.

The Old Testament books of Jeremiah and Ezekiel are filled with prophecies about the Babylonian Empire and its evil king, Nebuchadnezzar, who defeated Jerusalem and took the people captive. The Book of Daniel was written several hundred years after the Babylonian captivity; but Daniel makes Babylon a symbol for Israel's present oppressors, the Seleucid Empire. (The Seleucids were a family of Syrian kings who ruled a portion of the Alexandrian Empire of Greece.) John follows this pattern in the Book of Revelation, choosing the best-known enemy to God's rule, Babylon, as a thinly veiled symbol for imperial Rome.

John's dependence on the Old Testament prophets also goes beyond using this pattern, for the sayings about Babylon (Rome) in chapter 18 are similar to those spoken by Jeremiah and Ezekiel against Babylon and other nations. (Read Jeremiah 51 and Ezekiel 26-27 as you prepare to study Revelation 17–18.)

Perhaps the most common Old Testament metaphor for idolatry is sexual immorality, especially harlotry or prostitution. Israel was surrounded by people who had many gods. Many of these were female deities, and often the cults surrounding these female figures required deviant sexual practices and encouraged prostitution.

In contrast with its neighbors, Israel's law did not allow prostitution in any form. This statute, along with other laws of a similar nature, did much to preserve the dignity of sexuality.

The God of Israel required absolute loyalty. Throughout its history Israel's greatest struggle was with the temptation to tolerate or even nurture the worship of other gods. Israel's devotion to one God, YHWH, is sometimes portrayed by making YHWH the husband and Israel his bride. Against this background, we can see how infidelity might become a metaphor for idolatry. To worship other gods, was, in other words, to commit adultery against God, the bridegroom of Israel. The Old Testament prophets reflect on this imagery at length. One point they make is that Israel has behaved like a prostitute and committed adultery (Jeremiah 3:1, 6, 8; Ezekiel 16:15-22; Hosea 4:15).

The perspective shifts a bit in Revelation. Rome—consistently called Babylon—is a notorious provider of religious cults and gods. John does not address Israel or the church in these chapters but turns his prophetic eye for the first time directly on Rome, the source of idolatry and oppression against the church.

Revelation 17:1. John is less clear about the details of the visionary setting here than he is elsewhere. The voice doing the speaking throughout chapter 17 is one of the seven angels introduced at 15:6. The best solution to the question "Which one?" is that the seventh angel (16:17-21) continues on from the seventh plague to take the destruction of Rome one step further. (Rome is the object of the seventh plague.)

The influence of ancient prophetic writers on John is neatly illustrated in the title "the great prostitute, who sits on many waters." The prophet Nahum called Nineveh the "prostitute" (Nahum 3:4); Isaiah called Tyre a "prostitute" (Isaiah 23:16-17). Rome's location in the Mediterranean area does make some sense of the phrase *many waters*, but the phrase applies more aptly to the original Babylon that was surrounded by the Euphrates River, canals, and natural marshes. Jeremiah addressed Babylon as "you who live by many waters" (Jeremiah 51:13). The detail concerning many waters will create some difficulty when the symbol is interpreted in Revelation 17:15 as "peoples, multitudes, nations and languages." Thus we see two strands of meaning attached to one metaphor, a fact not unusual in Revelation.

Revelation 17:2-6. The image of the inhabitants of the earth being intoxicated with the wine of the prostitute's adulteries is enforced with the powerful image of verse 4. Babylon clutches a golden cup, a beautiful vessel, filled with obscene and filthy sexual practices.

Sexual immorality in all these references must always be taken at two levels that, as we have seen so often in Revelation, are so intertwined as to be inseparable: idolatry and ritual sexual immorality. The cup of Babylon's immorality will return in 18:3, 6.

Babylon not only makes others drunk but also is drunk herself. Her drunkenness is from the blood of those she has cruelly murdered. This ghastly image is established with absolute clarity. John expresses rage—passionate indignation—over the senseless killing of people. This issue will remain important in the minds and hearts of Christians for the next hundred years or more. Eventually, Christians wore down the Roman Empire by the spiritual and moral strength they demonstrated. The Christians' victory was, in part, made possible by the universal outrage over Rome's cruelty to people.

Notice the subtle word play going on throughout the latter half of Revelation. The wine of sexual immorality being hawked by the prostitute, Rome, is contrasted with the cup of God's anger, containing the wine of divine wrath (14:8; 15:1, 7; 16:1). These two cups have a close connection that borders on the dangerous. Both wines are a passion. The prostitute's passion is sexual immorality; God's passion is, to the forces of evil, the wrath and anger of punishment. Both are passions; one is impure, the other pure. John is reminding his readers that passion is part of existence. The only question is the motivation and direction that passion takes.

Revelation 17:7. John's use of the word *mystery* is rare (1:20; 10:7; 17:5, 7), even though many people consider Revelation mysterious. A more frequent term is *sign*, meaning a clarifying event or pronouncement. In John's Gospel, a sign is a miracle done by Jesus that makes understanding and faith in him possible for some persons. In Revelation, *mystery* means something of great significance that needs explanation. The meaning of *mystery* in Matthew, Mark, and Luke is almost the opposite. The kingdom of God cannot be explained but must be received in the person of Jesus Christ, who is God's mystery (see Matthew 13:11; Mark 4:10-12; Luke 8:10).

The woman and the beast on which she rides need careful explanation so the Christians to whom this vision is entrusted will better be able to know what is going to happen and how to deal with it.

Revelation 17:8-14. The interpretation of several phrases in this section has a long history of debate. The first is at the end of verse 8: "[The beast] once was, now is not, and yet will come." The meaning of this ambiguous phrase is, "The beast was alive, but is no longer living, and will once again appear." A similar idea is found in an equally confusing phrase in verse 10, where the mathematics of the seven kings is worked out. Out of the seven kings, five have passed from the scene, the sixth king is now reigning, and a seventh king is coming into power who will be around for only a short time. But verse 11 is by far the most potentially confusing. John has managed to get eight kings out of seven by suggesting that one of the kings will reign twice. Likely, John's description refers to the sea beast with seven heads, one of which was wounded but now has been healed. This reference may be to the Roman emperor Nero, who was thought by many to have returned to rule in the person of the emperor Domitian.

John likely had worked out who these kings were in the Roman succession. Many people have tried to reconstruct this list from general historical knowledge about the Roman Empire. They have come to no agreement about this list. One common solution would see the first five kings as (1) Augustus, (2) Tiberius, (3) Caligula, (4) Claudius, and (5) Nero. The sixth would be Vespasian and the seventh the short reign of Titus (AD 79–81). Titus led the Roman armies that destroyed Jerusalem and the Temple in AD 70. In this reconstruction, John and his churches are living under the cruel emperor Domitian (the eighth king), who many thought to be the reincarnation of Nero. In this scheme of things, then, an eighth king is really the fifth king returned to life.

Another solution would place John and his first readers as living under the reign of Nero. Thus Nero is the villain of the church in both cases.

The danger of specifying any such solution is that the power of the metaphor is robbed of its possibilities for all time. So we would be unwise to concentrate a great deal of attention on the historical accuracy of this list or others.

The ten kings represented by the ten horns (17:12-14) are a different matter. They almost certainly have no exact equivalents in John's mind. Rather, the portrayal is of what will take place in the final battle with Christ. These kings will be incited by the power given them by Satan. They will receive a sense of unity and purpose, but only for a short, bloody encounter with Christ. This final encounter is described in Revelation 19–20 and concludes with the Final Judgment.

Revelation 17:15-18. Even though the angel invited the prophet to view the "punishment of the great prostitute" (17:1), her judgment is not described until chapter 18. The strategy for Rome's destruction is suggested in 17:16-17. Rome will incite the nations to wrath; and the ten (minor) kings, led by Satan, will rebel against Rome and destroy her. The kings will then turn on Christ and be destroyed (17:13-14).

Some persons have suggested that Revelation belongs to a kind of literature that sees two equal forces—good and evil—at war in the universe. The language of verse 17 clearly makes such a conclusion impossible. God has access to the inner motivations of both kings and demons and manipulates their actions to bring about the divine outcome. God is in charge, and God is good.

Revelation 18:1-3. Now the judgment of Babylon comes. This entire chapter is written from the future perspective looking back. Rome, in the prophet's mind, already lies in ruins. Destruction is an accomplished fact. John learned this perspective from the Old Testament prophets, but it is more than a literary device. The entire perspective reflects an attitude of total confidence in the vision entrusted to the prophet. Thus John gives us a lesson for faith implicit in what may otherwise be seen as merely a literary technique. God is so powerful and dominant that the future can be seen as the past.

Revelation 18:4-8. Anyone who has read the great Old Testament prophets will be struck by the countless echoes from the prophets as this passage is read. This echo effect reminds us that Babylon is a timeless and elastic image for a limitless number of places and times.

Babylon's revealing statement of self-delusion is a powerful source of reflection (18:7). All persons living in protected luxury at some time are tempted to say, "I shall live forever, and nothing bad can happen to me." Nations and groups, too, in what they decide and do, proclaim, "Nothing can stop us. No adversity will deter us; nothing will stand in our way." The Book of Revelation is of great importance for the support it provides in stripping off the mask of self-deceit.

Revelation 18:9-10. The kings who have gathered to lament Babylon's destruction are all the lesser kings bound to Rome through conquest and alliance. This is not, in all probability, the group of ten kings mentioned in 17:12-14.

Revelation 18:11-19. Read Ezekiel 27:12-36, which is the model for Revelation 18:11-19. As the list of import and export trade items grows, so does an atmosphere of cynicism. We are chilled to realize that these merchants mourn only the loss of trade and care nothing for Babylon. This picture is extremely powerful, for in their words of mourning, the merchants and seafarers condemn themselves. Babylon has managed to create mutually degrading relationships. This situation is the certain result of greed and manipulation at work.

John concludes the list of trade items with "human beings sold as slaves" (v. 13). The Roman Empire was built with the labor and craft of slaves, an especially cruel chapter in Roman history. Even though some Romans worked, with some success, to improve the outrageous conditions under which slaves often had to serve, slavery was the cruel, dark side of Rome's glory.

Revelation 18:20. Rejoicing over Babylon's destruction may also seem cynical and cruel. We must be clear about a distinction in this regard. People of God, apostles, and prophets are called to rejoice because God's judgment has triumphed, not because a great but cruel kingdom has fallen. Since God's judgment is always just, that judgment cannot possibly result in evil. God cannot do injustice. The careful reader will notice in Revelation that not once does anyone complain that God has acted unjustly.

Revelation 18:21-24. When Jeremiah spoke his oracle against the historic Babylon, he was asked to dramatize his message by taking what he had written; binding the scroll to a stone; and casting it into the river Euphrates, which flowed through the center of Babylon. The meaning of this prophetic act was, "So will Babylon sink" (Jeremiah 51:63- 64). Something quite similar happens here.

This part of John's vision ends with a verbal walk through the ghost town that was "the great city." Remarkably enough, a quick walk through the ruins of the forum in Rome today can recapture a great deal of the atmosphere suggested by John's description. The great irony of these two chapters is that, while Rome was destroyed by marauding armies, it fell, not as a pagan empire, but as a Christian nation. Between the time of the writing of Revelation and Rome's final destruction, Rome had been converted to Christianity.

DIMENSION THREE: WHAT DOES THE BIBLE MEAN TO ME?

Revelation 17–18

(NOTE: Participant book has questions related to 17:1-6a, 15-18; 17:6b-14; 18:1-18, 19-24.) Let us not oversimplify the theological perspective of these two chapters in Revelation. We have seen in other parts of this book a depth of perspective that does not encourage a quick identification of evil with *them* and of righteousness with *us*. The development of thought in these chapters is unusually dependent on vast parts of the Old Testament prophetic inheritance. A careful reflection on this fact will make it apparent that the same invectives leveled against foreign nations such as Babylon were leveled also against Israel.

We have suggested in this lesson that Babylon is an elastic, universal image for the danger of self-deception and idolatry. Because idolatry is close to the center of the biblical notion of all that is essential to human sin, Babylon can be a parable about us and our institutions. We see every day in our news contemporary examples of Babylon spinning out.

Should we ever rejoice over the defeat of another person, movement, or nation? We must be cautious in making such judgments. When the righteous are called by God to rejoice over Babylon's fall, we could easily conclude that this applies to other circumstances in which what we know to be evil is defeated. The difference is, of course, that the conclusion is drawn by God. The parable within the parable of these chapters could be that our quick judgments about whom and what is evil may be examples of our own self-deception and self-idolatry.

"Hallelujah! / Salvation and glory and power belong to our God." (19:1)

11

THE SWORD OF HIS MOUTH

Revelation 19–20

DIMENSION ONE: WHAT DOES THE BIBLE SAY?

Answer these questions by reading Revelation 19

1. Why does the multitude praise God? (19:2)

   They praise God because "true and just are his judgments" and because "he has condemned the great prostitute" and thereby avenged the martyrs.

2. Who else praises God? (19:4-5)

   The twenty-four elders, the four living creatures, and all God's servants also praise God.

3. What is the topic of the hymn sung to God? (19:6-8)

   The hymn is about the coming marriage of the Lamb to the bride.

4. What does the angel say when John tries to worship him? (19:10)

   The angel tells John not to worship him, since the angel is "a fellow servant with you and with your brothers and sisters."

5. What are the names given to Christ? (19:11, 13, 16)

   Christ is called "Faithful and True," "the Word of God," and "KING OF KINGS AND LORD OF LORDS."

6. What does Christ come to do? (19:11, 15)

   Christ comes "with justice" to judge and make war on the nations.

7. To whom does the angel call, and what does he order them to do? (19:17-18)

   The angel calls the birds to come eat the flesh of the armies gathered to do battle with Christ.

8. Who has gathered to do battle? (19:19)

   The beast and "the kings of the earth and their armies" gather to battle "against the rider on the horse [Christ] and his army."

9. What happens to the beast and the false prophet? (19:20c)

   They are captured and "thrown alive into the fiery lake of burning sulfur."

10. What happens to the kings and their armies? (19:21)

    They are slain by "the sword coming out of the mouth of the rider on the horse."

Answer these questions by reading Revelation 20

11. What happens to Satan? (20:1-3)

    Satan is thrown into the Abyss for one thousand years.

12. During this one thousand years, what happens to those who have conquered Satan's forces? (20:4)

    They sit in authority with Christ.

13. What happens to the "rest of the dead"? (20:5)

    The "rest of the dead" do not come to life until the thousand years are ended.

14. How does John describe those who are raised? (20:6)

    They are the blessed, the "priests of God and of Christ."

15. What happens after the one thousand years? (20:7-8)

    Satan is loosed from prison, and he deceives the nations (Gog and Magog). They all gather for battle.

16. What happens to this huge army? (20:9)

    As they surround the camp of God's people, fire from heaven destroys them.

17. What happens to Satan? (20:10)

    Satan joins the beast and the false prophet in the lake of fire and sulfur forever.

18. What is the next event? (20:11)

    John sees God appear on a "great white throne."

19. Why has God come? (20:12-13)

    God has come to bring to life all the dead and to judge them.

20. How is this judgment done? (20:12)

    God consults the book of life and "the books" to find out who is listed in the book of life and what they have done.

21. What happens to death and Hades? (20:14)

    Death and Hades are "thrown into the lake of fire."

22. Who else is thrown into the lake of fire? (20:15)

    Anyone whose name is not found in the book of life is thrown into the lake of fire.

DIMENSION TWO: WHAT DOES THE BIBLE MEAN?

Revelation 19:1-8. The descriptions of heavenly worship are central to the structure of Revelation. As we approach the last scene of worship in Revelation, we should reflect on this dimension in the book.

No other New Testament book includes such sustained interest in worship, poetry, music, liturgical response, and captivating visual symbols. This observation suggests to me a comparison with the Old Testament. The story there is quite different. Not only does the Old Testament present entire libraries of poetic prayers (Psalms) and other kinds of poetry (Proverbs, Ecclesiastes, much of the writings of the prophets), much of the Old Testament is devoted to describing places of worship such as the tabernacle and the various temples in Jerusalem. In other words, both the means of worship (prayers, rituals, buildings, vessels, songs) and acts of worship occupy an enormous part of the Old Testament.

Revelation is steeped in the Hebrew Scriptures. Revelation contains direct references to nearly all the books of the Old Testament. But John seems to have been most deeply impressed with the Torah (or Mosaic law), the books of poetry related to worship and wisdom, and the writings of the prophets.

This brief overview shows clearly that Revelation is not a book that represents the extremist margins of the Jewish-Christian tradition. The truth is that Revelation draws more evenly in its theological depth from all parts of the Old Testament than do most of the New Testament books. The impression that John knows only Ezekiel and Daniel is created by the fact that he draws on these books in a sustained, repetitive way not seen anywhere else in the New Testament.

The importance of liturgy and liturgical elements in the Book of Revelation is evident. This emphasis is the result of John's cultural circumstance. While we as free citizens of a democratic nation have difficulty understanding John's circumstance, we need to try to capture the feeling that comes from being captive, oppressed, and without options.

Imagine what it is like to be surrounded by strong enemies, ruled by foreigners, fed and housed at the whim of a despot, told precisely what to do and what not to do. In these circumstances, one's view of reality can change dramatically. Jews and Christians have experienced these circumstances at various times. When they have done so, their religious ideas have changed to sustain them in their seemingly helpless situation. In these times of periodic oppression, the worship of God has surfaced as the all-important aspect of existence. Many factors can explain this increase in the importance of worship, but the most important is the need for the human to be caught up in the uniqueness of the divine.

The inner dynamic of this response of worship can be described in this way. Imagine that all around us are the visible and real signs of power, which limit what we do and say, where and how we live and move. This power attempts even to determine what we think. We can do nothing to change this power structure. Our freedom to flee is curtailed. To resist is possible but laughable in practical experience. We have no chance but to survive and persist in our survival.

We must see, somehow, another reality that draws us beyond the limitations that mere survival supports. This other, unseen reality can begin to take a form that can defeat the apparent realities of physical, political, and economic oppression. For Jews and Christians this reality has been the sovereignty of God, who controls all history as Creator. If God is seen as king, then this king must have a court, a ritual, and a means for followers to pay homage. The court, ritual, and homage paying is worship and the "stuff'" of worship. In the liturgy of worship, we are caught up in the reality of God's sovereign role, and in this reality all else is placed in a new perspective.

This experience may be hard to comprehend in its potential power to reorder our perception of an otherwise desperate circumstance. Our difficulty in understanding it, however, does not deny the fact that millions have learned to live in this way. The hymns and liturgical responses of Revelation are not simply pretty poetic statements that beautify the text. Rather, the worship of the Lord God Almighty invites into a new realm of existence those whose lives are tragically restrained by earthly realities of cruel oppression.

We are not describing *escapism*. Escape is the denial of reality, however momentary and brief the denial may be. The elements of Revelation, so reminiscent of the hymns in Psalms, Isaiah, and Ezekiel, describe another reality that can be made real only by the praise of God in worship.

Revelation 19:9-10. In verse 9, the angel is not inviting the people to the Lamb's marriage supper. The Lamb—the risen Son of God—both invites persons to and hosts this feast. This distinction creates a gateway of insight into a basic concept in John's thought. Christ is both the means and the sign of God's redemption. If, through God's intervention in history, only a great prophet had been sent to convey the message of God's love, the prophet would have been a means of salvation. However, the figure of Christ as sign also gives a particular revelation of God's love that could have been communicated in no other way. Christ, as God's definitive sign of love, is hinted at in the subject of the section, the invitation to the marriage supper.

No mention could be made of the Lamb's wedding feast without directly inferring the Lord's Supper. The sacrament of the Lord's Supper is made possible by the death of Christ (as Lamb of God), and the cross gives meaning to this sacrament. At its simplest, Holy Communion represents Jesus' act of love at Calvary. We could even say that Holy Communion proclaims the cross. But the representation of Holy Communion awaits fulfillment. The marriage supper of the Lamb is, therefore, Holy Communion made complete. Whereas, in our present celebration, we seek to have Christ made present by the sacrament; at the conclusion of history, Christ will be really present with the faithful. The image of marriage suggests the people of God being united or joined with Christ, who has been separate since his death and resurrection.

Revelation 19:11-21. John has conveniently divided this section into three parts (19:11-16, 17-18, 19), creating three small visions laid side by side to form a kind of triptych (three-hinged panels whose pictures tell a religious story). The first panel (19:11-16) describes Christ as a mighty warrior-prince whose terrible appearance convincingly conveys the certainty of victory. The next panel (19:17-18) presents an interlude cleverly disguised as a call to birds of prey in which the outcome of the battle is gruesomely described even before it begins. The third panel (19:19) shows the pitiful preparations of the beast and the false prophet. The three panels end with a surprisingly swift and clean stroke, drawing together the first two panels into one statement: "The rest were killed with the sword coming out of the mouth of the rider on the horse, and all the birds gorged themselves on their flesh" (19:21).

Revelation 20. This chapter is best thought of as describing three epochs and events. In 20:1-6, the thousand-year rule of Christ is described; in 20:7-10, the battle of Gog and Magog is narrated; and 20:11-15 describes the final resurrection of the dead and the Last Judgment.

All three sections contain important ideas and descriptions. For many people, Revelation 20 is of sole importance, especially those people who live in a state of preoccupation with the "signs of the end." They look at Revelation 20 for clues about what may be happening in the near future. However, centuries of Christian reflection on Revelation have led to a significant and broad conclusion that you, as leader, need to consider carefully. The accumulated wisdom is this:

1. When interpreters try to put the names of nations, individuals, and events in history on symbols, images, and scenes described in Revelation, one can be certain that the interpretation is headed in the wrong direction. Thousands of people have tried to add names to these symbols; all have failed.

2. A second element in this collective wisdom is that when elaborate and complex doctrines are extracted from brief, even sketchy, passages in Revelation, one can be sure that the doctrine is evidence of human ingenuity and not necessarily the Bible's viewpoint. When texts from Revelation are plucked from their native setting and joined together in a complex web of proof texts from completely different parts of Scripture, one should be cautious, perhaps even skeptical, of using such interpretations. The Bible does have an astounding unity in spite of its great theological diversity. But the unity is not of a sort that fits well with the finely tuned doctrinal developments that have taken place in the nearly two thousand years since Revelation was written. Those who try to make Revelation fit with a doctrinal inheritance are treading on dangerous ground.

3. Finally, those who are aware of the long and often tangled history of Revelation are better suited as guides. If you find a book or article that makes no reference to this history and does not discuss it critically, be wary. These cautions are offered to you in the event that you wish to research more fully some of the ideas in this chapter and elsewhere in Revelation.

Revelation 20:1-3. The *Abyss* is a favorite image in Revelation (9:1, 2, 11; 11:7; 17:8). John is well aware that hearers could easily become confused by his cast of "bad actors." Therefore, he makes it clear that the evil influence being chained in the Abyss is none other than the arch-demon, Satan. Satan is described by four names (20:2): the dragon, that ancient serpent, the devil, and Satan. John makes the power of evil in the world more believable by his infrequent references to Satan. Rather, Revelation demonstrates that evil has many forms and that the most dangerous are the subtle ones. All the agents and influences of evil have been removed when the beast and false prophet are cast into the fiery lake in 19:20. They will remain there forever and be joined later (20:10) by Satan. However, for the present interlude, Satan will be restrained, not destroyed—restrained for a period of a thousand years.

Revelation 20:4-6. The thousand years is not to be taken as a literal time in history but as a period symbolic of restoration. The period of a thousand years is often called "the millennium," taken from the Latin words for "one thousand" and "year." The millennium has been discussed and argued since the first centuries following the writing of Revelation. The concept was defended by such notable scholars as Irenaeus and Justin Martyr. However, the concept of a literal millennium, together with elaborations shaped into a doctrinal position, became associated early with various movements held to be heretical. Millennialism dropped from sight for several centuries and was revived first among the churches of the "Radical Reformation," for example the Anabaptists and Moravians. Millennialism was also a center of focus for the pietists of Germany and was, therefore, a common idea in various German Brethren groups.

Actually, the description found here is quite general and sketchy. The broad picture is that Satan is chained and without influence. Therefore, a period of renewal takes place on earth. The most important aspect of this period is the implied link with the Creation story in which life in Eden is without conflict, suffering, or hardship. In a sense, Eden is restored, and creation is in harmony as it once was. A "new creation" of humans happens as well. This new Eden is populated by the faithful martyrs described in 7:9-10, 13-14. These are raised from the dead in a kind of limited resurrection. The faithful from this period are given a special privilege. They can enjoy the presence of Christ in a world without evil.

The broad outlines of such a restoration have firm roots in scriptural tradition, found, not so much in the New Testament, as in various strands of the Old Testament, especially in the prophets of the exile. The description found in Ezekiel 40–48 is one example, which John will draw on from this point of Revelation to the end of the book.

Revelation 20:7-10. Gog and Magog are taken from Ezekiel 38:1, 9, 15. For Ezekiel, this unified symbol was a veiled reference to Babylon, in whose hands Israel lay captive. For John, as we have seen, Babylon is Rome. Often in Christian history, "Gog and Magog" have been identified with contemporary nations or oppressors. Some people still try to identify them today.

The description of the battle and its preparations is parallel with that of 19:17-21 and ends in the same way. With the final destruction of Satan, the way is paved for the event prior to the final creation of a new existence by God.

John obviously wrote Revelation with an eye on the Genesis account of Creation. The Eden narrative concludes with the human and environmental condition of the world vastly altered by the act of human disobedience inspired by "that ancient serpent" (20:2). With Satan destroyed, a new creation is possible.

Revelation 20:11-15. With the description of the judgment before the great white throne, we are returned to the vision of God's throne in Revelation 4–5. The various visions of judgment described throughout this book began with that vision. Christ, standing before the throne, broke the seals of the scroll and set in motion God's judgment. That judgment is brought to conclusion here. Thus the circle is completed. In this cycle everything begins and ends with God's sovereign rule. God is the Creator who must follow to perfect completion that which is created. The general resurrection described here is, in effect, a second creation of humankind. In the next chapter, we will see the new creation brought into existence by God. In this sense, the placement of Genesis and Revelation within the Christian canon of Scripture is a profound statement.

While not all parts of Scripture witness to a belief in a general resurrection from the dead, Revelation is not alone in this faith. A more detailed description of this ancient understanding is found in 1 Thessalonians 4:13-17 and 1 Corinthians 15. The same is true of the Final Judgment. A more elaborate description is offered by Matthew 25:31- 45. Both of these examples of parallel belief illustrate also the reason for not basing detailed doctrinal views on Revelation 20. In 1 Thessalonians 4:17 and 1 Corinthians 15:51- 52, Paul clearly believes that many of his fellow Christians will still be alive at the time of the resurrection, a view not suggested in Revelation. Again, Matthew 25:31-45 clearly has Jesus Christ ("the Son of Man") as the primary agent in the Final Judgment. The Gospels of Mark and Luke support this idea. In Revelation 20:11-15, however, the prophet John does not mention Jesus Christ. I do not see this as a problem of contradiction. Rather, this example shows how foolish it is to base the points of doctrine on single passages of Scripture.

A particular and impressive idea in our passage is that death and the dwelling place of the dead, Hades, are conquered by this resurrection. Death surrenders its captive dead. This act is a hint that death is viewed as a separate reality that must be conquered. One could even say with Paul, who paraphrases Isaiah 25:8, "Death has been swallowed up in victory" (1 Corinthians 15:54). This suggestion is strengthened by the fact that death and Hades are cast into the fiery lake. This striking image of death being condemned to death will permit John to envision in the new heaven and earth a place where "there will be no more death" (Revelation 21:5).

DIMENSION THREE:
WHAT DOES THE BIBLE MEAN TO ME?

Revelation 19–20

(NOTE: Participant book has questions related to 19:1-10, 11-16, 17-21; 20:1-10, 11-15.) The participant book poses several questions that may cause problems for group members. Spend some extra time reflecting on these questions. You might consult a pastor or theologian to discuss some of the questions with you or with the group members.

Christian pacifists have thought a great deal about the rather frequent use in the Bible of God and Christ as warriors who lead in the fight against evil. You may wonder how pacifists can accept such an image in light of their commitment to peace. These Christian thinkers have concluded that this biblical problem poses little, if any, incongruity. Even as a warrior, God is still God and not tainted by the injustice that almost always accompanies our decisions to act aggressively and make war.

I believe that any war in human history can find its ultimate cause in national idolatry, greed, prejudice, and misunderstanding. However, when God is portrayed as making war (as Christ and God both are in these chapters of Revelation), God is acting on behalf of pure justice. We cannot say that the battles portrayed in 19:17-21 and 20:7- 10 are based in the justifiable grounds of self-defense. Nor are these scenes based on a "just-war" theory in which Christ must defend the righteous from the vicious attacks perpetrated by evil forces. Rather, war in these passages is a metaphor for the struggle between good and evil.

The easy identification of nations with good or evil in the history of earthly wars has been a large part of the problem humans have had to live with for centuries. Do not allow this distinction to guide the discussion of these chapters in Revelation. John was thinking of historical events and nations when he wrote. As we pointed out in lesson 10, however, the destruction of Rome did not bring about the end of the world. We are much better off to think of this evil as a metaphor for human sin.

We live in an age of terrible possibilities that would result from war, especially nuclear war. It is more important that we seek to understand the possible results of earthly war than to speculate about which are the good and evil nations of our age.

Another aspect that may raise problems in the discussion of this lesson is the interest many people have in "the millennium." I have emphasized in this lesson the fact that the millennium has been a minor part of the church's message of salvation. Some groups and individuals, however, seek to make this concept a complex and essential part of belief. The majority of Christianity has focused in another direction, all the while not seeking to deny or reject the faith of those who use the Scripture as a main tenet for their faith in the millennium.

The claim that Christ or God will rule over a final judgment of all who have ever lived is quite another matter. This claim is found in all parts of the New Testament and in the historic creeds. The issues involved in God's judgment that lead to the punishment of some are much the same as the issues involved when God is seen as a warrior. Notice that Revelation 20:15 is a conditional sentence: "Anyone whose name was not found . . ." The precision with which the sentence is written deserves a similar precision in pondering its meaning. One interpretation is clearly excluded by this precision, that in some predetermined way any particular person is excluded from the book of life.

We cannot escape from the fact that judgment is an inevitable part of God's justice. However, the unifying motif of the Bible is that God's grace seeks to redeem, not to destroy.

Many persons believe that all deeds—good and bad—are kept in a kind of ledger that is somehow "totaled up" at some time in the future. This view is not encouraged by Revelation 20:11-15, even though you could easily draw that conclusion. What we do is certainly important, but inclusion in the book of life is not based on human goodness. Read Revelation 21:5-8, which is an excellent commentary on 20:11-15. There you will see that the gift of life is "without cost," freely given by God (21:6c).

"I am the Alpha and the Omega, the Beginning and the End." (21:6b)

12

I MAKE ALL THINGS NEW
Revelation 21

DIMENSION ONE:
WHAT DOES THE BIBLE SAY?

Answer these questions by reading Revelation 21

1. What happens to our heaven and earth in John's final vision? (21:1)
    "The first heaven and the first earth had passed away" to make room for a new heaven and a new earth.

2. What does John see "coming down out of heaven from God"? (21:2)
    He sees "the Holy City, the new Jerusalem, coming down out of heaven."

3. What image does John use to describe "the new Jerusalem"? (21:2)
    John describes the new Jerusalem "as a bride beautifully dressed for her husband."

4. Who first speaks to John in his vision? (21:3)
    John hears "a loud voice" speaking from the throne of God.

5. What is the message from the "loud voice"? (21:3-4)
    The voice announces the advent of God. God will dwell with humans as a community. God will comfort all anguish; and death, pain, and grief "will be no more."

6. Who speaks next? (21:5a)
    God speaks directly to John.

7. What does God command John to do? (21:5b)

John is to write down the words God will speak, for they are "trustworthy and true. "

8. What is the message John is to write down? (21:6-8)

God is the cause and conclusion of all things. God freely offers the gift of "the water of life." God exhorts the readers to overcome and thereby to inherit the gift of life. God also pledges to be God and Father to those who are victorious. The message concludes with a warning to avoid sin, lest their inheritance be the fiery lake.

9. Who appears next in John's vision? (21:9)

One of the angels with the seven bowls full of plagues appears next, possibly the same one who spoke to John before in 17:1.

10. What does this angel want with John? (21:9)

The angel wants to show John the bride of the Lamb.

11. What does John see from the "mountain great and high"? (21:10-11)

John sees "the Holy City, Jerusalem, coming down out of heaven from God" and shining with radiance like a precious jewel.

12. How does John describe the Holy City? (21:12-14)

The city's dimensions are symmetrical. Twelve foundations inscribed with the names of each of the twelve apostles support a great high wall that surrounds and makes up the city. This wall has three gates in each of its sides. Each of the gates is inscribed with the name of one of the twelve tribes of Israel. Posted at each of the gates is an angel.

13. What does the angel do next? (21:15)

With a golden measuring rod, he begins to measure the city.

14. What description comes from this measurement? (21:16-17)

The city is a perfect cube, being the same dimension in height, length, and depth.

15. What is the city made of? (21:18-21)

The city and its streets are made of pure gold. The walls are made of jasper and the foundations of precious stones. The twelve gates are made of pearls.

16. Is there a temple in the city? What form does it take? (21:22)

The city has no temple, for "the Lord God Almighty and the Lamb are its temple."

17. What else is missing, and why? (21:23-24)

"The city does not need the sun or the moon" to shine, since light comes from the glory of God.

18. Who is drawn into the city by its light? (21:24, 26)

The nations of the earth and their kings come to the city and bring their splendor with them.

19. Is the city open? (21:25)

Apparently so, since the city gates are never shut in the daytime and "there will be no night there."

20. Who can and cannot enter the city? (21:27)

"Those whose names are written in the Lamb's book of life" are permitted to enter the city. Those who do what is "shameful or deceitful" are excluded.

DIMENSION TWO:
WHAT DOES THE BIBLE MEAN?

Background. This chapter is one of the great landmarks in all Scripture. Suggesting that one or another part of Scripture is more or less important than other parts can be dangerous. Without the totality of Scripture we would not be able to guide our decisions and our faith. Still, the history of the use of Scripture by the church has clearly marked off Revelation 21 as a milepost in biblical theology. Why is this? We can identify several reasons.

1. Without this chapter, much of the admittedly confusing parts of Revelation would not be as clear. An example of this is the extended metaphor concerning the prostitute of Babylon, as we will see in detail later.

2. Many of the historic disputes concerning Revelation's interpretation are reducible to this question: Does Revelation present a master scheme for understanding the full scope of cosmic and human history, or is Revelation a treasure house of images and insights that apply to all places and times? Revelation 21 presents the holy city as trans-historical, implying that one ought not to force the parts of Revelation into a rigid map for historical events.

3. The theological depth of the ideas and metaphors of Revelation 21 is so rich as to defy exhaustion by human creativity. This chapter has more treasure per square inch, so to speak, than we usually find in other short chapters of the Bible.

4. God's absolute dedication to justice is seen throughout Revelation, but often God's justice is shown in its condemning dimension rather than in its redeeming mode. In Revelation 21, the final word is one of invitation to enter the heavenly city and freely receive the grace of God. This emphasis is so clear as to be unmistakable. While present in other parts of Revelation, this aspect of God's justice must be uncovered by careful reflection. Thus Revelation 21 draws the book toward a grace note that sets the rest of Revelation in a quite different light.

5. Revelation 21 not only presents a unifying vision of God's intentions for the incarnation of Jesus Christ; it also brings into union with Christ the highest visions of hope found in the Old Testament. In this way, Revelation is a clarifying statement of the salvation theme seen in all Scripture. Few places in the Bible contain such a statement. The unity of redemption's proclamation is symbolized by God's self-revelation as the beginning and end (Alpha and Omega) of all things. If God is the cause and the conclusion of all existence, then unity is necessarily limited to God's intention for all things. Revelation 21 presents God as seeking the unity of all times, peoples, and circumstances by means of entering the city of God.

Revelation 21:1-4. The frankly feminine image of the bride of Christ in Revelation (19:7; 21:2, 9; 22:17) invites comparison with other female images in Revelation. The "woman clothed with the sun" (chap. 12) is one, and the prostitute of Babylon (chaps. 17–18) is another. I can find no clear correspondence between the bride of the Lamb and the woman of Revelation 12. The figure in chapter 12 is clearly a mother, not a bride. The woman's role there is to give birth to a child, who in turn will create an entire people. The prostitute of Babylon, however, is a different matter. John almost certainly places the harlot and the bride side by side for purposes of deep theological significance, a dichotomy that, while perhaps effective, is likely one foundation for the stereotypical portrayals of women in literature throughout history.

In concrete terms, the prostitute is Babylon, or Rome. The bride is the new Jerusalem. Neither should be limited in our minds to historical realities in time and space. Rather, both figures are extended metaphors of limitless dimensions that provide deep and rich possibilities for reflection. Babylon and Jerusalem represent the two dimensions of human possibility. The prostitute seeks to seduce with the wine of idolatry; the bride seeks to glorify the true God of light who fulfills the glory of human potential. The power of these two images is drained if they are seen as other than ourselves. As an example of John's boldness in Revelation, all cities, all institutions, all movements, at different times, can be the prostitute of Babylon or the bride of the Lamb. To claim otherwise would be an example of the idolatry John speaks against.

In 13:11-17, we came on the astounding figure of a pseudo-lamb, a creation of the beast, who became the priest of the beast's image. This religious leader functioned precisely by means of creating a beast cult that used every appearance of the true faith in a clever but ruthless way. The cult featured a dead but resurrected image in imitation of the Lamb who was slain and raised from the dead. The deceit that the pseudo-lamb works is a parable for the constant threat of self-deceit in the Christian community. How else would the cleverest priest of evil work than by imitating, with credible precision, the elements of the true faith? To make this statement is much the same as saying that the new Jerusalem is in constant danger of playing the harlot of Babylon. This recognition may not be comfortable, but the threat is only increased if the insight is denied.

This correlation between female images is given more detail later in chapter 21 when much is made of the kings of the earth streaming to the light of the city of God to bask in its glory (21:24). As we read this verse, we are reminded of the funeral lament of the kings of the earth at the death of the Babylonian prostitute. When the kings of the earth, who committed adultery with her and shared her luxury, see the smoke of her burning, they will weep and mourn over her. Terrified at her torment, they will stand far off and cry: "Woe! Woe to you, great city, / you mighty city of Babylon! / In one hour your doom has come" (18:10)!

The artistic positioning of these two women/cities is a clear message to all the nations of the earth: to follow Babylon may, for a fleeting moment, create what kings, merchants, and artists proclaim "great"; but the attachment is false and fatal. True glory for a people is to rejoice in the light of God, the incarnate temple of the eternal city, the new Jerusalem.

As with all great images, the comparison of Babylon and Jerusalem can enlighten many human experiences. Revelation is clear that every Christian congregation can turn from spotless bride to drunken prostitute without even noticing the difference. Several of the mini-letters of chapters 2–3 contain this idea. While at first we may think that suggesting the church can become Babylon's prostitute is heretical, John makes it plain that to claim anything else is the most pitiful kind of heresy. (Of course, wisdom and history teach us that we do not have a license for determining when this heresy has taken place; quite the reverse. When we begin to suspect other groups, we are, ourselves, in real danger of idolatry.)

The "loud voice from the throne" (21:3) also spoke in 19:5. The voice announces the outcome of the marriage of the Lamb and his bride. The point of marriage is union. This union is the completion of Christ's redemption in the formation of a community.

The clothing of the bride in 19:8 is the fine linen of righteousness, more closely defined as "the righteous acts of the saints." When paired with the negative list in 21:8, we see that the quality of the bride in Revelation 21 is that of moral righteousness. Take care not to read moralism into this text. John does not say that by moral righteousness the bride becomes "the wife of the Lamb." Rather, the point is that righteousness characterizes the people of God.

Revelation 21:5-8. The affirmation that God's words are "trustworthy and true" is characteristic of Revelation. Christ is described in Revelation 3:14 as "the faithful and true witness" and in 19:11 as "Faithful and True." God's ways and judgment are called *true* in 15:3 and 16:7. Why are these adjectives chosen? Revelation is, in essence, the unmasking of falsehood. John points out that daily we meet false Christs, false prophets, and false gods. In the deceit of evil, truth is the first victim. In the eyes of John, the first element of victory for believers is to recognize the truth. Recognizing the truth is not presented as an easy task. Rather, seeing the truth is a struggle in itself. Victory follows when the lie is unmasked and truth triumphs.

In the chaos created by evil's deceitfulness, the call to conquer evil is really the same as the call to recognize the truth. Since God is true, finding God's words in the abundance of other words becomes essential to victory. The trustworthiness of God's words relates to a different dimension of Revelation's thought world. Throughout these pages, we find a description of the untrustworthy character of nations, cults, and religious and political leaders and ideas. The search for that which is trustworthy—that which is reliable and dependable throughout the test of time—is much like the search for truth. The declarations of God are as trustworthy as the words that brought the universe into being. The same One who caused all that exists, says John, is reliable as Sustainer and Perfecter of that creation.

Using words that describe God as Creator and Sustainer should not surprise us in light of the constant claim that the words that John is commanded to write are, quite literally, the words of life (1:3; 22:7, 9, 10, 18, 19).

John refers to an unceasing source of life for the Christian, as does the writer of the Gospel of John. In conversation with the Samaritan woman at the well, Jesus proclaimed, "Whoever drinks the water I give them will never thirst. Indeed, the water I give them will become in him a spring of water welling up to eternal life" (John 4:14). In Revelation 7:17, Jesus Christ is described as the Lamb and the shepherd who will guide the faithful to "springs of living water." Possibly John is speaking of Christian baptism here. However, this reference should not be thought of as the ritual of baptism. Rather, the inner meaning of baptism is at stake. In John's theology, Jesus Christ is the sacrament of baptism and Holy Communion. Without Christ these sacraments would be empty forms.

Water as a symbol of life will be presented later in a beautiful passage (22:1-6) with the description of living waters flowing from the throne of God and the Lamb. The point of the images in both chapters is that God in Christ is the Source of life. This fact is a present reality and possession, not simply a future hope.

The list of moral failures in 21:8 may sound familiar, but none of these descriptions appears earlier in Revelation. (However, the similar description "those who practice magic arts, the sexually immoral, the murderers, the idolaters," and liars is repeated in 22:15.) Here persons are described by the immoralities to which they are devoted. Thus idolatry is really the fundamental sin.

Revelation 21:9-14. From this point forward, Revelation is deeply influenced by Ezekiel, especially the vision of a restored, physical temple—Jerusalem—and territory for the twelve tribes. This vision begins in Ezekiel 40 and fills the next eight chapters. When John is carried by the Spirit "to a mountain great and high" (Revelation 21:10), he is reliving Ezekiel's experience (Ezekiel 40:2). (In the Bible, mountains are often the sites of great revelations, as in the lives of Moses, Elijah, Ezekiel, and Jesus.)

John's emphasis on the walls and foundations of the new Jerusalem clearly has theological interest. The holy city of God is not constructed in a vacuum. Rather, the entirety of salvation history becomes the base for the city. This base reminds us that the tradition of the patriarchs and apostles contains the essential understandings for Christian reflection. A process of decision making that seeks the truth but neglects the tradition of Scripture is built on an unstable foundation. At the time of Revelation's writing, Christians did not have a New Testament. The New Testament canon was not decided until many years later. The foundation of the twelve apostles, therefore, is the apostolic confession cherished by the church even before the New Testament came into existence. Therefore John is living within the boundaries of a received tradition.

Revelation 21:15-21. Further difficulties occur with this list of precious stones. Quite frankly, no two English translations agree at every point in translating the Greek words for these stones. The problem is essentially archaeological. We cannot know in some cases what stone was called by what name in different cultures of the world.

A possible source for the list of precious stones is the description of Aaron's breastplate in Exodus 39:8-14. However, the lists do not correspond in name or in order. Precious stones are significant throughout the Bible as a means of revealing the mysteries of God.

The most important dimension of these precious stones is clear, however. Only the apostolic tradition faithfully conveyed to believers is a reliable foundation for a faith that will stand. Because this apostolic tradition concerns God, Christ, and the Holy Spirit, the faith of those who confess the Father, Son, and Holy Spirit will triumph over other, less reliable forms of revelation. If John has added an element of playfulness to his list of stones, the playfulness is intended to show the unreliability of other revelations of supposedly eternal truths.

Revelation 21:22-27. John gives us a gift in that no temple appears in the city of God. With a temple, this vision would simply be a hope for the restoration or perfection of something that once was—precisely the point of Ezekiel's vision. By emphasizing that God and the Lamb *are* the temple, John lifts his sights beyond the banal realities of historical limitation. The point is this: If the holy city can be identified with a particular geography and nation, then all those who wish to be a part of the city must become resident aliens in that time and place. John's vision of the holy city recognizes the timeless quality of the presence of God. The temple of God is ultimately portable; it exists wherever God and the Lamb are proclaimed.

Glory best describes the presence of God in John's theology. This distinctive idea is a constant theme in Revelation. On virtually every page, we find angels, martyrs, saints, and the peoples of earth engaged in praising God's glory (e.g., 1:6; 4:9, 11; 5:12-13; 7:12; 11:13; 14:7; 19:1, 7). Glory is an idea with great depth in Revelation. As we have pointed out, the most appropriate human activity in Revelation's view is the praise of God's glory, or put another way, the glorification of God. This activity is appropriate because God is the Creator of all that is. Therefore, when we (the creature) glorify God, we place in the proper perspective the ordered nature of existence.

Glorification makes possible the proper perspective on all dimensions of life. For example, we tend to try to control as much of existence as possible. But what is appropriate to human control and what is not? In many situations, this question becomes quite complex. The act of seeking to glorify God has the potential to clarify many of these difficult decisions. John does not suggest that the glorification of God is limited to speech. Rather, acts resulting from decision making are a part of the glorification of God. For example, those who wear the white robes in chapter 7 glorify God. They are identified as martyrs, those persons who by conscious decision refused to compromise in any one of a number of possible ways and were put to death for their belief. Nor does this viewpoint seek to make otherwise complex issues overly simplistic. The glorification of God is seen as a constant, dominant factor in the daily task of speaking and acting in love.

The mention of *light* and *lamp* in 21:23-24 is important. John shows a sustained interest in images of light in Revelation. In the first vision, Jesus was seen standing in the midst of the "golden lampstands" (1:12-13). Then the churches are seen as "golden lampstands" (1:20). In 21:23, the Lamb *is* the lamp. Since complete unity exists between God and the Lamb, however, God is also the city's light. *Lamp* and *light* are metaphors for a revelation. Jesus Christ, as the Lamb of God, brings clarity to human existence. Christ does this by revealing God's love in his act of a death freely accepted.

Why the emphasis on this dimension of Christ here? The answer reveals the profound beauty of Revelation's thought world. The goal of the Christian community, existing in all places and in all times as the city of God, is not survival but mission. The city exists to transform, to proclaim, to serve, and to grace all other cities of the world.

John also speaks of an earthly glory and honor. The kings of the nations are not belittled for the glory they possess. However, this glory and honor will never be complete until they are united to the supreme glory that belongs only to God.

The mention of nations serves several purposes. The apostolic witness gave importance to the faith of Christ as available for all peoples of the world. The struggle of the apostolic age was to present the Christian movement as a universal and frankly missionary reality. Revelation here brings this same message. The sweep of this vision is quite breathtaking. Rather than minimize the true accomplishments of nations, John presents an image that comprehends and congratulates these achievements. He also presents these achievements with a loftier reality.

Revelation 21:27 repeats a theme found often in the book. John hates all that is false and deceitful (14:5; 22:15). All that is false is not of Christ (16:13; 19:20; 20:10) because truth is found in Christ. In what is a typically circular way of thinking, Christ is truth; therefore evil can only create doubt in the minds of the faithful and others by deceiving them about the truth.

DIMENSION THREE:
WHAT DOES THE BIBLE MEAN TO ME?

Revelation 21—Moral Righteousness

(NOTE: Participant book has questions related to vv. 1-4, 5-14, 15-21, 22-27.) Some of the questions in the participant book are quite complex. For example, the New Testament itself struggles at length with the question of Christian morality. We learn from the Gospels that Jesus proclaimed and required a life of moral righteousness. The apostle Paul is clear that even if we were capable of living lives of moral righteousness, such activity would not earn us salvation (Romans 10:1-9). This belief has caused many persons to ask, "If we are required to be morally righteous but that righteousness does not win us salvation, why then be good, or even try to be good?" The perspective of covenant and the terms of the covenant can help us answer this question.

We could say that the history of God's dealing with humankind from the beginning of creation is characterized by the gentle and loving invitation of God to the people of God to enter into a meaningful relationship. This relationship is frequently described as a covenant.

By *covenant* we mean that pledges and faithfulness to those pledges are offered on the part of God. Furthermore, both parties in this covenant have obligations. Mutual obligations, however, do not suggest an equal relationship. God's initiative in establishing the covenant with us is based on a level of love and commitment that we can never equal. Still, all persons and communities brought into this covenant are expected to live in faithfulness to the relationship of the covenant. High on the list of these obligations is the attempt to live in a way faithful and consistent with our vision of God's righteousness.

We could say, then, that all righteousness belongs to God and our obligation is to live within that righteousness: to seek it, enable it, live by its light, and promote its concerns. This obligation is often called "the love demand." The covenant demands of us that we live in a way consistent with the love that brought the covenant into being. Another way to put this is that we must imitate God's perfect love.

God's love is seen in its fullness in the way by which God calls people to the covenant. The premium example of God's love, of course, is the gift of the Son of God in the incarnation, Jesus Christ. Within the incarnation of Jesus Christ, the clearest measure of God's love is seen in the Passover death of the Lamb of God. In gratitude for this gift and this display of redeeming love, Christians seek to be faithful to the vision of righteousness. This faithfulness, in essence, is the biblical understanding of the reason we joyfully respond to Christ's call for moral righteousness.

Anyone who carefully reads the Revelation to John could never make the mistake of thinking that such moral righteousness is the basis of salvation. John is exceedingly clear that one of the fundamental flaws in the human creation since the Fall is the constant tendency to establish our own creation as our idol. This idol is quite often the product of our own creativity and inventiveness.

This premium sin of idolatry is reflected most clearly in our attempt to use righteousness as a basis for bartering with God for salvation. Since this bartering is clearly an attempt to place God under the obligation to act according to the terms we establish, it is also clear that it will never work. Not only is righteousness a free and undeserved gift from God, it is also a demonstration of the true nature of our creation as human beings.

One of the great paradoxes of human existence is that the life lived under the demands of love is also the most satisfying and happy life. This paradox is true, but not because acting in love is always easy. Nor does it suggest that the way of love is without suffering and misunderstanding. In fact, the way of love is demanding and frequently leads to personal and corporate suffering. However, the way of love remains the most satisfying and happy existence because it is the way that human beings were intended to live. In part, satisfaction comes from the single-mindedness and wholeness that result from this way of life. While we cannot prove this fact empirically, it has been demonstrated biographically for hundreds of years in the lives of saintly persons, both celebrated and anonymous, since the beginning of the Christian vision.

Revelation 21—The City of God and the Church

People are often disturbed by the suggestion that the church is not always identified with the city of God. The church, as a gathered community of saints, often permits the light of God to shine through its life of active witness and verbal proclamation. At other times, the church's witness rings like a bell made of lead, and darkness seems to prevail in all its pronouncements. The church given by Christ is, of course, a heavenly reality that is sometimes clearly evident in the earthly organization of the church; at other times, this reality seems not to be present at all. John's vision of the holy city clarifies this perspective. For him, the holy city of God is the dominant divine reality in all existence, without limitations of time and space. This heavenly reality can be totally earthly and human and can also escape the human grasp. This reality redeems John's vision from being something from another realm and time but with no bearing on the present. However, the search for the holy city of God is never-ending and must be engaged day-by-day in each generation.

As you discuss this vision with group members, try to make your questions and issues as open and creative as possible. This vision is virtually limitless in its potential. By it we are called to a life that need not be limited by our sense of powerlessness, by the manifestations of history, and by our self-imposed limitations to see the presence of God in our midst. In many ways, this vision is comparable to others in Scripture that lift and elevate the human spirit. The vision has its own genius because the metaphor is so close to the reality of daily existence. Try to help group members see these creative possibilities in your discussions.

"Blessed is the one who keeps the words of the prophecy written in this scroll." (22:7b)

13

THE HEALING STREAM
Revelation 22

DIMENSION ONE: WHAT DOES THE BIBLE SAY?

Answer these questions by reading Revelation 22

1. What is the source of the remarkable river shown to John in the vision? (22:1)
   The river comes from "the throne of God and of the Lamb."

2. What is this river's course? (22:2a)
   The river flows through the main thoroughfare of the city of God.

3. What is remarkable about the tree of life? (22:2bc)
   The tree has fruit on it perpetually, a different kind each month. Its leaves have healing properties.

4. How does John describe the city of God? (22:3)
   The city is a place for the worship of God and the Lamb. There is nothing cursed in the city of God.

5. What are the two privileges given to those who dwell in the city of God? (22:4)
   They are permitted to view God's face, and their foreheads are inscribed with God's name.

6. What has God done for God's servants? (22:6b)
   God has sent an angel to show the servants what must take place soon.

7. According to the message given to the prophet John, what event is foretold? (22:7a)
   The near approach of Christ's return is foretold.

8. Who is given a special blessing? (22:7b)
   Anyone who keeps the words of the prophecy written in "this scroll," the Book of Revelation, is blessed.

9. By what name does the author of Revelation identify himself? (22:8a)
   He gives his name simply as "John."

10. The angel warns John not to do what? (22:10)
    John is warned not to seal up the words he has written.

11. Who is to remain in the same condition in light of the nearness of time? (22:11)
    All people, evil and righteous, holy and vile, are to remain the same.

12. What will Christ and God do when this happens? (22:12)
    All will be repaid for their deeds.

13. Who is blessed, and what do they receive? (22:14)
    Those who have washed their robes are blessed, and they will have the right to enter the city and use the benefits of the tree of life.

14. Who must live outside the gates of the city of God? (22:15)
    Those who practice many kinds of unrighteous acts: magic, adultery, murder, idolatry, and falsehood.

15. How does Jesus describe the book that John has written? (22:16a)
    He calls it a "testimony for the churches."

16. By what names does Jesus identify himself? (22:16b)

    He calls himself the "Root and the Offspring of David" and "the bright Morning Star."

17. Why are all persons who are thirsty invited to "come"? (22:17)

    They are called so that they may drink from the water of life at no cost.

18. What are the warnings given to all who might want to change the words of Revelation? (22:18-19)

    Those who add to it will be plagued; those who subtract from it will be barred from the city of God and the tree of life in it.

19. Who is it that witnesses to the words of Revelation, and what does he say? (22:20a)

    It is Jesus; and he says, "Yes, I am coming soon."

20. How does John respond to these words of Jesus? (22:20bc)

    He affirms the pledge of Jesus to come soon and spontaneously says, "Amen. Come, Lord Jesus."

DIMENSION TWO: WHAT DOES THE BIBLE MEAN?

Revelation 22:1-2, 17. Viewed even in realistic terms, water is fundamental to life. As we have followed the visionary description of judgment in Revelation, we have seen frequently that the destruction and contamination of the earth's water supply and seas creates horrific conditions for not only humans but also the partner creatures of earth (8:8-11; 16:4). Conversely, God is the source of life-giving water in both the real sense (14:7) and the spiritual (7:17; 21:6). It is no surprise, then, to learn that water or springs of waters is a metaphor for God's essence. This is especially true in the poetic visions of the great prophets.

Isaiah envisions the day when "with joy you will draw water / from the wells of salvation" (Isaiah 12:3). Jeremiah weaves an extremely artful oracle from this same image. In the extended metaphor of 2:13, he rebukes the people of Judah for rejecting God, "the spring of living water," in favor of the contaminated water of "broken cisterns," a clever reference to idols made of clay. The remarkable point in Jeremiah's words is use of an image that virtually creates a title for God: the Spring of Living Water.

Throughout the Old Testament is the foundational notion of water being the source of life, not only by nourishing humans, beasts, and fields but also in originating creation. This view lies in the shadows of the Creation account of Genesis 1:2, where the Spirit of God "hovering over the waters" implies that water must be dealt with first as the primal matter of creation's work. Water does not have to be created; it is the stuff of life before life has form. However, Scripture makes it evident that God is in control of water. The threat that water can impose is first seen in the Flood, and this theme continues in many parts of the Hebrew Scriptures. Only because God is sovereign of all that exists do the waters of the earth and from "under" the earth pose no threat.

Against this background, something of the full extent of the idea in Revelation 21 and 22 takes on full shape. Notice, for example, that the water of life flows from the throne. The participant book points out that the point of origin establishes with finality that God and the Lamb are the primal sources of life. In fact, this idea is closely connected with the original Creation story. In the beginning, God created life by moving over the deep. This creation is never-ending. God continues to create life. Thus, water is only an incidental sign for the creation of life. Of course, the life spoken of here is more than physical existence. Rather, a quality is projected that is not simply "future life" but that which is given in the present and will persist into the unknown future.

The metaphor of the tree(s) of life is quite another matter. Nowhere else in Scripture is God compared to a tree, probably because of the idolatrous practices of Israel's neighbors. For example, Jeremiah derides those who say to a tree, "You are my father" (Jeremiah 2:27). However, there is a clear link with the veritable orchard in the garden of Eden and one particular tree, also called "the tree of life" (Genesis 3:22, 24). To the extent that the gates of the city of God are thrown open to give access to the tree(s) of life, Eden is again open to the human creation. Notice that this is, however, not a fully developed presentation in which the paradise of Eden is systematically reconstructed.

Finally, the careful reader will notice some minor confusion in the text. Whereas the tree of life in 22:2, 19 is consistently singular, the description of the city of God clearly envisions the river lined with many trees on both banks. This may not be confusion at all but simply evidence of the dual influence of Genesis 3, in which there is one "tree of life," and Ezekiel 47:1-12, in which there are many trees lining the banks of the river.

Revelation 22:3, 6, 9. John's understanding of himself, of the angel who guides him, and of those in the churches to whom he writes is based on the common biblical idea of *servant*. It is one of the most frequently repeated associations to say that the prophets are God's servants. Those who are called the servants of God in the Old Testament include Moses, David, Job, Sarah, Jacob, and countless others. In fact, the covenant nation of Israel is portrayed as the servant of God (Isaiah 44:1). Jesus is identified by Matthew as the servant of God, using the words of Isaiah 42:1-4, one of the great servant songs. "Here is my servant whom I have chosen, / the one I love, in whom I delight" (Matthew 12:18). In the view of both the Old and the New Testaments, the people of God are a company of fellow servants called and sustained by the Lord of the universe. In the eyes of the New Testament, this company is led by the example of a Master Servant (no contradiction in terms of biblical thinking): "Who, being in very nature God, / did not consider equality with God something to be used to his own advantage; / rather, he made himself nothing / by taking the very nature of a servant" (Philippians 2:6-7).

Only Revelation deals satisfyingly with a distinct problem in this common theme, how servanthood can be kept from its degrading connotations. This is accomplished in the consistent theme of worship. The throne of God is surrounded by countless creatures of God's creation. They are unified in their unceasing praise of the Creator. Praise of the Creator is the most appropriate expression of one's recognition of the nature of both God and creation; the full divinity of personhood is made possible by means of worship. The point, therefore, of servanthood is not the debasing of angels and humans but the commonality of creatureliness.

The problem of our difficulty with the concept of servanthood is also connected with a more distinct theme in the Gospels. There, the point of being a servant is following the example of Christ, who demonstrated the inner meaning of servanthood by the final act of service, his own death: "Whoever wants to become great among you must be your servant, and whoever wants to be first must be slave of all. For even the Son of Man did not come to be served, but to serve, and to give his life as a ransom for many" (Mark 10:43b-45).

Revelation agrees that *service* is the essence of servanthood, but the book broadens the scope of *service*, redefining its core. In Revelation, *service* is, quite simply, the worship of God. However, we must not limit this to our idea of what constitutes worship. The worship of God means honoring the Creator of life in all ways, including the search to complete the command to love our neighbors with all our being.

We could well ask what, precisely, the idea of worship adds to the notion of service. We find several dimensions to the answer by reading Revelation carefully. The most important of these concerns the motivation for service. Service, interpreted by worship, is not something that can be externally commanded, but, rather, is a spontaneous expression. The many scenes portraying worship around the throne cannot be read in any other way. These narratives convey, unmistakably, that the throngs who are in the presence of God cannot refrain from their liturgical responses. Another way of saying this is to affirm that worship is love in action. The response of love is discussed in the letter to Ephesus (2:2-7). There, the church members are praised for all they do and hold dear but are warned that they have abandoned the love (*agape*) that they had at first. Set in the context of praise for all else, this at first appears to be a strange criticism. After all, if the Ephesians are doing everything well, what could be criticized? Perhaps the abandoned love here is that sense of immediacy, single-mindedness, and spontaneity that must characterize commitment to Christ.

Revelation makes it clear that, in times of testing, inadequately based morality will be the first to go. If worship is the most authentic human response, then worship is also the factor most likely to sustain a life of service. Service to God and neighbor is the best way to live because living a life of service is consistent with God's creation. This explanation may sound circular in reasoning, but it is necessarily so.

The classic problem in our tradition is, "Why should I love my neighbor as myself?" While we might be tempted to respond with answers that describe the structure of obligation ("Because God says you ought to love"), these will not ultimately satisfy most. The very particular answer from Revelation is quite different: You love God and neighbor because you recognize in the acts of love the fullness of your own creation. Other kinds of answers occur in Scripture, but this answer from Revelation has a special kind of beauty that deserves greater attention. Notice that the rationale I have outlined above does not suggest that we serve others in order to be happy. This would be a distortion, if not a perversion, of Revelation's view. Rather, John suggests that service, seen in the light of worship, is the authentic response of love that, in turn, is cohesive with and affirming of our creation.

Finally, when service is seen through the prism of worship, its joyful aspects are seen most clearly. Service done grudgingly, whether in the chapel or on the street, quickly becomes capable of doing more harm than good. Recapturing the joy of service often happens when we join in the spiritual worship of God. Conversely, all authentic worship will result in service to neighbor.

Revelation 22:7, 12, 20. This chapter is heavily punctuated by affirmations of the return of Christ in the very near future. What are we to make of this claim in light of the intervening centuries in which Jesus has not returned? Does this fact alone make void the entire Book of Revelation? This problem is significant and one that the group members will almost certainly want to discuss, perhaps to the exclusion of all other topics.

The Book of Revelation stands somewhat apart from the Synoptic Gospels (Matthew, Mark, and Luke) in one aspect. In Revelation 22:20, John reports Jesus saying, in the first person, "I am coming soon." Jesus never said those words in the Gospels. More characteristic would be this statement from Jesus in Mark 13:32-33: "But about that day or hour no one knows, not even the angels in heaven, nor the Son, but only the Father. Be on guard! Be alert! You do not know when that time will come."

The emphasis in the Gospels is on diligence and watchfulness, since the precise time of Christ's return is unknown. We can also presume that Jesus meant to convey uncertainty about whether the time would be *soon* or *distant*. Most scholars assume that Jesus and his followers thought that this second coming would be sooner rather than later. Thus it would seem that there is an essential difference between the Jesus of the Gospels and of Revelation. It is quite one thing to imply the speedy return of Jesus in glory and quite another to have Jesus say the words, "I am coming soon."

The entire atmosphere of Revelation is replete with this sense of urgency. The very word *soon* is common in Revelation (2:16; 3:11; 11:14; 22:7, 12, 20) but never used in the Gospels in connection with apocalyptic events. The fact is that Revelation comes from a particular viewpoint that is credible and significant, and one without which the New Testament would not be complete. This viewpoint stems from the condition of many Christians living under vicious, sustained oppression. If we were to live under these conditions daily, we would likely also come quickly to the affirmation that Jesus is coming soon. In fact, this context is really the correct one for reading such statements as that of Revelation 22:20.

The final statement is a spontaneous cry from the prophet's heart (and notice that this verse is the first time his own prayers have been allowed to intrude in the text): "Amen. Come, Lord Jesus!" The confession that Jesus is coming soon is then a prayer caused by the real experience of a church under the heel of naked power and the threat of death.

A note of caution should be carefully reflected on at this point in our study. One of the unfortunate historical developments that grew out of this quite particular emphasis on the speedy return of Christ was the attempt of various persons to convince others that Jesus had already returned (in, perhaps, a hidden or disguised way). This development has persisted into modern times, and we can be sure that it will be tried again.

This provides an occasion for celebrating the fact that we have the whole Bible for our careful study and reflection. For example, Mark's "little apocalypse" takes a very cautious approach to this question, giving a helpful and practical guideline to deal with the problem spoken of above: "If anyone says to you, 'Look, here is the Messiah!' or, 'Look, there he is!' do not believe it. For false messiahs and false prophets will appear" (Mark 13:21-22a). This guideline needs to be kept clearly in the group discussion; for while much the same point is made by Revelation, the point is not as explicit and clear as in Mark's warning above.

Finally, this question of the speedy return of Christ must conclude, always, with the plain affirmation that Christians have from the beginning and must continue to live in the light of our historic faith. At a time unknown and in ways unexpected, God will act in Christ to bring an "Amen" of perfection to existence as created.

Revelation 22:7b-14. Revelation has seven beatitudes (1:3; 14:13; 16:16; 19:9; 20:6; 22:7b, 14). Two are found in this chapter. The first (1:3) and sixth (22:7b) blessings are given to those who give careful attention to the message of Revelation. A grave textual problem appears in the seventh blessing (22:14). Some texts of the Greek New Testament say that "those who wash their robes" are blessed, while others bless those who "obey God's commandments." The New International Version is probably correct in choosing the first translation. Revelation speaks elsewhere of keeping the commandments of God (12:17; 14:12) and also of washing robes (7:14), so both ideas are credible in the context of the book as a whole. However, placing the admonition to "obey God's commandments" here looks as if it has been added from 12:17 and 14:12 to create a moral mandate more fitting to the context (22:11-12).

Revelation 22:16. This description of Jesus is reminiscent of John's Gospel and the many "I am" statements made by Jesus there. While the self-description of Jesus here ("I am the Root and the Offspring of David, and the bright Morning Star") may sound familiar, it is not. Nowhere else in the New Testament is Jesus called the "Root of David," except in Revelation 5:5. Both Matthew and Paul know the prophecy of Isaiah 11:1, "A shoot will come up from the stump of Jesse." This prophecy was interpreted to mean that Jesus was the fulfillment of prophetic hopes, Jesse being the father of David, and Jesus being born into the lineage of David (Matthew 1:6 and Romans 15:12). But the affirmation here (22:16) is quite different and also typical of Revelation. To say that Jesus is both the Root of David and the Offspring of David is much the same as to say that Christ is "beginning and end" (Alpha and Omega). Rather than being a shoot from the stump of Jesse, Christ is the root of Jesse's stump.

In Revelation 2:28, those in Thyatira who keep the works of Jesus to the end will be given "the morning star." Taken with this verse (22:16), we could say that the gift in mind is a portion of Jesus Christ, who is the Morning Star. While stars figure highly in the images of Revelation, it is startling to have Jesus given this name. The only connection within the New Testament is in Matthew 2:2; the star of the East giving direction to the magi is described by them as "his star."

Revelation 22:17. The bride of Christ, we learned in 21:2, is the city of God. The picture portrayed here, then, is of the Spirit and the holy city inviting all hearers of Revelation to "come." Revelation is a book of invitation. The persuasive word *come* is used frequently (4:1; 6:1, 3, 5, 7; 11:12; 17:1; 19:17). More difficult to identify, however, is the third party who says, "Come." Who is "the one who hears"? This third party must be the reader. This identification is confirmed by the next sentence, which is a further invitation to "the one who is thirsty" and "the one who wishes [to] take . . . the water of life." In this gentle and sensitive literary movement, the reader is now invited to take part in the action of the text. The city and its contents have been described. The reader is now invited to share in its potential and its bounty. These gifts are "free," that is, both priceless and without need to be purchased. This sense of salvation as the free gift of grace repeats 21:6c and is consistent with the entire New Testament witness.

Revelation 22:18-19. This warning is fascinating in light of Revelation's textual history as well as the history of its interpretation. While this leader guide has not made much of the technical details, you should know that Revelation has the most difficult and disputed text in the New Testament. The task of establishing, with even a modest degree of certainty, the original text of the Greek manuscript has exhausted the energies and talents of countless schools from the time of Jerome (347–420). We have often commented on the history of interpretation and the extent of misuse and abuse to which this book has been unfairly subjected. This problem continues to the present. Added to this is the early dispute about whether Revelation should even be included in the Christian canon. All these facts give a poignant irony to John's words of warning.

Overall, I must say at the conclusion of our study that we neglect the positive values of Revelation at our own peril. In spite of the difficult and checkered history of Revelation, its message has persisted and prevailed. Again and again, Revelation has been "rediscovered" and rescued from abuse by those who find in it a message that speaks to some in a way found nowhere else in Scripture and yet that agrees with the witness of all Scripture.

DIMENSION THREE: WHAT DOES THE BIBLE MEAN TO ME?

Revelation 22

Because Revelation is a complex book, you will certainly want to review with the group the major and dominant themes that have arisen in your discussions. Among these may be the notion of sin and deceit presented so profoundly in Revelation. You may also want to discuss the view of Christ as the Lamb, the only one worthy to open the sealed scroll; the glimpses of early church life provided by the seven letters in chapters 2–3; the call to endurance of the saints living under the domination of the evil city of Babylon (Rome); the hope offered in John's vision of the holy city, the bride of Christ; the other beautiful poetic images and descriptions of John's vision; and the focus on worship as our ultimate service of God and the Lamb.

As a closing for your final session, you might want to offer the benediction John provides in 22:21: "The grace of the Lord Jesus be with God's people. Amen."

Made in the USA
Monee, IL
23 January 2020